AF427099

Legacy

Testimonies of Faith, Hope and Love.

Lydia and Bill Maeda

Copyright © 2024 **Live The Difference**

All rights reserved. No part of this publication may be reproduced, distributed, or transmitted in any form or by any means, including photocopying, recording, or other electronic or mechanical methods, without the prior written permission of the publisher, except in the case of brief quotations embodied in critical reviews and certain other noncommercial uses permitted by copyright law. For permission requests, write to the publisher, addressed "Attention: Book Rights and Permission," at the address below.

Published in the United States of America

ISBN 979-8-89395-758-7 (SC)
ISBN 979-8-89395-756-3 (Ebook)

Library of Congress Control Number: 2024921815

Live The Difference
P.O Box 9143
San Bernardino ca 92427
lydia@legacylivethedifference.com

Ordering Information and Rights Permission:

Quantity sales. Special discounts might be available on quantity purchases by corporations, associations, and others. For details, contact the publisher at the address above.

For Book Rights Adaptation and other Rights Permission. Call us at toll-free 1-888-945-8513 or send us an email at admin@legacylivethedifference.com.

Dedication

We would like to take this moment to dedicate this book to our family. Our family is a living testimony of the restoring power of Jesus Christ. We lived in the realm of suffering and we have walked out the path of restoration. Through all the trials and tribulations, we have demonstrated, the heart of a champion. We have gone where we have never been and we have accomplished what we never thought we could do. Through the power of the living God, all things were made possible. This book is dedicated to the memory of Monique. For all the lives that she touched, for every soul that was saved, for every person who experienced the love of God for the first time, may her legacy pass forth from generation to generation. To our Children who are and will continue to be our inspiration. To our parents Tony and Mary who supported us through thick and thin, and to my Mom Tsurumi who revealed to me what it really means to be a Dad. We Love you. To my wife Lily, who fought the good fight, never gave in and never quit, you are the best part of me. I will love you for eternity and a day. To my husband Bill who stood by me, through all the ups and downs, being my ladder carrier, wiping the tears, and for speaking life into me. I love you with all my heart

Lydia and Bill Maeda

Contents

Dedication iii

Acknowledgements vii

Introduction ix

   There is Hope ix

Chapter One 1

   A Mother's Loving Memory 2

Chapter Two 9

   A Born Leader, Still Teaching 9

Chapter Three 21

   Wise Beyond Her Years 21

Chapter Four 35

   Praising God 35

Chapter Five 43

   A Heart that Inspired and Motivated Others 43

Chapter Six 57

   Always Sharing God's Peace, Love and Joy 57

Chapter Seven 67

   The Smile that Lives Forever 67

Chapter Eight 73

   When Words are not Enough 73

Chapter Nine 87

   The Real Deal 87

Chapter Ten 97

    A Family Affair 97

Chapter Eleven 109

    Monique's Legacy 109

Chapter Twelve 131

    Memories for a Lifetime 131

Chapter Thirteen 139

    Letters to Monique 139

Conclusion 171

    Learning to be more Christ-Like 171

    Today 174

    Hope-yes there is….. 177

About the Authors 182

Acknowledgements

As years have passed, we have faced the giants of fear, doubt, denial and sometimes disbelief. Now we bathe in the living waters of restoration as we pass from glory to glory to glory. We would like to first and foremost thank our Lord Savior Jesus Christ, who supplied us with the belief and divine inspiration, that all things are possible, yes including writing a book. Many people have helped us along the way but for following people we would like to express a special acknowledgement. Thank you Yara Tiznado and Loretta Peer for your proofreading skills and your constant prayers and encouragement. Lita Ramirez who has been our constant friend, voice of reason and prayer warrior. Gilbert Flores for securing and creating the website. This acknowledgement would not be in order if we did not express our sincere thanks to Joe and Loretta Peer who stood by us through the darkest moments of our lives. For every tear there was a hug. For every moment of sorrow, when there seemed to be no adequate words to fill the void of emptiness, just a smile and a pat on the back was more than enough. For never trying to minister to us or to say something profound, just loving on us and excepting where we were on the road to restoration. When we were being told to pull ourselves up by our bootstraps, and to get on with life, you just loved us. Thank you for your demonstration of a God kind of love, finally to Eddie Ferguson who through his financial contribution, and personal belief, this book would not have been possible.

$\mathcal{I}$ntroduction

There is Hope

***"May the God of hope fill you with all joy
and peace as you trust in him, so that you
may overflow with hope by the power of the
Holy Spirit."***

—Romans 15:13 NIV

The Bible is filled with passages of hope. Peter tells us that we should praise God for granting us a living hope. Peter 1:2-4: "Praise be to the God and Father of our Lord Jesus Christ! In his great mercy he has given us new birth into a living hope through the resurrection of Jesus Christ from the dead."

Death might be easier to bear if our loved ones did not first have to physically die before being reborn to their spiritual bodies in Heaven. It is a price we pay because of Adam's sin. Yet, God, in His infinite wisdom, has chosen not to allow us to simply become dust, but to raise us up to share His Kingdom with Our Savior.

When a family experiences tragedy, especially the loss of a child, their faith is tested to the extreme. These are the times when we must remember the words of our Savior and cling to His promise and hope. We will be reunited with our loved ones in Heaven. When the Lord calls a child home, it is easy to allow grief to become so overwhelming that it can lead a person to becoming self-centered. Instead of sharing grief and seeking comfort with another person, the individual's pain becomes a beacon, drawing the person inside where he or she picks apart the heart in misery, shutting out a spouse, and, sometimes, other still-living children.

This often leads to the break-up of a marriage, destroying the beautiful relationship and sacred bond that God has entrusted to the couple. Although our faith was sorely tested, and at times, we seemed to be losing the battle, Monique's enduring love and faith reminded us of God's promise and hope and in the end, we persevered.

The loss of a child is a tragedy of epic proportion. Every facet of our lives was altered. It challenged the very core of our marriage, and sorely tested the stability of our family. As chaos infiltrated our home, God reminded us that losing a child was not an acceptable reason for either divorce or the disintegration of our family. Yet in the midst of our grief, these thoughts were fleeting considerations. Faith is a word easily spoken in the confines of church. But we did not understand the true meaning of faith until this tragedy attempted to overwhelm our lives. Faith gained an almost supernatural definition, as we realized the power that comes from real faith. We realized the plan and purpose of our lives placed before us. The simple question was would we seize it and run the race, or would we self-destruct, forever falling into a dark bottomless abyss?

Yes, we lost a child, and in dealing with this loss and the seemingly insurmountable grief, we nearly lost ourselves, struggling with the thought that we, her parents, had outlived our child. We were suffocating as we choked upon our own grief. Monique's passing was wrong, completely out-of-order. How could a child, who had so much to offer, be snatched from the arms of her parents? Often, God brought this into our remembrance, Isaiah 55: 8-9: "That my thoughts are not your thoughts, and your ways are not my ways, for as Heaven is higher than earth, so my ways are higher than your ways, and my thoughts than your thoughts". The answers to the questions we so desired would not be known to us, until we stood before the Lord. Life would continue with us or without us. There were moments when we chose to abstain from life, yet still, life continued. In the darkness of our room, we cried out to God for a reason, a simple answer as to why Monique went home. Yet, no answer was forthcoming, just the deadly quiet of our room, the rhythmic breath of my wife, as the hands of God captured her silent tears. The loss was very real.

In the midst of our loss, we realized that there was gain. What could we have possibly gained by the loss of Monique? We gained the revelation that there was no loss. Monique went back to where she came from. We will all go back to where we came from. We are all only on loan from the all-mighty God. Through Monique's passing God granted us a glimpse of eternity, allowing us to experience Heaven in a supernatural way. God set upon us, his knowledge, that Heaven is a real place and eternity is forever.

It is our desire and belief that you will find not only peace, but inspiration in life through Monique's testimony, personal memories, and the stories of those who knew her. We hope you will gain the understanding that it is possible to have a Christ like effect on the lives of others. Simply stated, we can touch lives in a 'Monique' kind of way. More importantly, it is not only our revelation, but hopefully, also yours, that life only begins on earth. For those in Christ will pass on to an eternal life—a permanent life in Heaven.

The Bible is filled with passages of hope. Peter tells us that we should praise God for granting us a living hope. Peter 1:2-4: "Praise be to the God and Father of our Lord Jesus Christ! In his great mercy he has given us new birth into a living hope through the resurrection of Jesus Christ from the dead."

Death might be easier to bear if our loved ones did not first have to physically die before being reborn to their spiritual bodies in Heaven. It is a price we pay because of Adam's sin. Yet, God, in His infinite wisdom, has chosen not to allow us to simply become dust, but to raise us up to share His Kingdom with Our Savior.

When a family experiences tragedy, especially the loss of a child, their faith is tested to the extreme. These are the times when we must remember the words of our Savior and cling to His promise and hope. We will be reunited with our loved ones in Heaven. When the Lord calls a child home, it is easy to allow grief to become so overwhelming that it can lead a person to becoming self-centered. Instead of sharing grief and seeking comfort with another person, the individual's pain becomes a beacon, drawing the person inside where he or she picks apart the heart in misery, shutting out a spouse, and, sometimes, other still-living children.

This often leads to the break-up of a marriage, destroying the beautiful relationship and sacred bond that God has entrusted to the couple. Although our faith was sorely tested, and at times, we seemed to be losing the battle, Monique's enduring love and faith reminded us of God's promise and hope and in the end, we persevered.

Loss vs. Gain

The loss of a child is a tragedy of epic proportion. Every facet of our lives was altered. It challenged the very core of our marriage, and sorely tested the stability of our family. As chaos infiltrated our home, God reminded us that losing a child was not an acceptable reason for either divorce or the disintegration of our family. Yet in the midst of our grief, these thoughts were fleeting considerations. Faith is a word easily spoken in the confines of church. But we did not understand the true meaning of faith until this tragedy attempted to overwhelm our lives. Faith gained an almost supernatural definition, as we realized the power that comes from real faith. We realized the plan and purpose of our lives placed before us. The simple question was would we seize it and run the race, or would we self-destruct, forever falling into a dark bottomless abyss?

Yes, we lost a child, and in dealing with this loss and the seemingly insurmountable grief, we nearly lost ourselves, struggling with the thought that we, her parents, had outlived our child. We were suffocating as we choked upon our own grief. Monique's passing was wrong, completely out-of-order. How could a child, who had so much to offer, be snatched from the arms of her parents? Often, God brought this into our remembrance, Isaiah 55: 8-9: "That my thoughts are not your thoughts, and your ways are not my ways, for as Heaven is higher than earth, so my ways are higher than your ways, and my thoughts than your thoughts". The answers to the questions we so desired would not be known to us, until we stood before the Lord. Life would continue with us or without us. There were moments when we chose to abstain from life, yet still, life continued. In the darkness of our room, we cried out to God for a reason, a simple answer as to why Monique went home. Yet, no answer was forthcoming, just the deadly quiet of our room, the rhythmic breath of my wife, as the hands of God captured her silent tears. The loss was very real.

In the midst of our loss, we realized that there was gain. What could we have possibly gained by the loss of Monique? We gained the revelation that there was no loss. Monique went back to where she came from. We will all go back to where we came from. We are all only on loan from the all-mighty God. Through Monique's passing God granted us a glimpse of eternity, allowing us to experience Heaven in a supernatural way. God set upon us, his knowledge, that Heaven is a real place and eternity is forever.

It is our desire and belief that you will find not only peace, but inspiration in life through Monique's testimony, personal memories, and the stories of those who knew her. We hope you will gain the understanding that it is possible to have a Christ like effect on the lives of others. Simply stated, we can touch lives in a 'Monique' kind of way. More importantly, it is not only our revelation, but hopefully, also yours, that life only begins on earth. For those in Christ will pass on to an eternal life—a permanent life in Heaven.

Chapter One

"Jesus said to her, "I am the resurrection and the life. He who believes in me will live, even though he dies;"

—John 11:25 NIV

When a parent loses a child, others will sympathize, especially other parents. They cannot help thinking, "What if that had been my child?" Compassion allows them to briefly touch the surface of the pain that is so overwhelming to the grieving parents. But unless they have actually experienced a loss themselves, their imaginings can only scratch the surface. Remembering the special times and characteristics of a child is not only natural, but in a sense, healing, as the parent shares the pleasures their child enjoyed, the way others saw and appreciated that boy or girl, the child's special talents, and even the funny and sad times.

Monique was a very special girl. It seemed that the Lord had filled her brief life with love, compassion, and a clear sense of right and wrong. She loved God and her fellow human beings so much that she could not help sharing that love with everyone she met. She accepted her lot in life and never complained that it might be lacking in material things—Monique was rich in all the ways that truly mattered most. God calls each one of us to search for the riches of Heaven over those of the earth. Jesus said that if we obey the first two commandments to love God above all others and to love our neighbor as ourselves, all of the rest would fall into place.

It seems that Monique, who only lived on this earth for fifteen years, got it right from the very beginning. Truly, she was an angel sent to bless the lives of others. Such devotion and dedication for one so young will continue to shine like a beacon for those who knew her. Take comfort and treasure your own children and all of their unique gifts, whether living here or in Heaven. God has blessed each of us with special talents. We honor Him when we use those gifts to the best of our ability, just as Monique did.

A Mother's Loving Memory

My daughter Monique was unique in every sense. She had many fine qualities as do all my children. However, she possessed one special attribute that even I, over the course of time, seemed to overlook—the way she expressed unconditional love.

Monique was just an average teenager to most people, including me. She had a love of music as well as dancing, favorite TV shows, and a unique style of dress. What set her apart was her ability to love others as she loved herself. Monique had an exceptional ability to see others as God would see them. She saw the good in everyone, and this allowed her to love as Jesus loved without reservation. Under some of the most difficult circumstances, she was able to overlook the negative. During these times of trial, our daughter was capable of finding the silver lining—the positive side of life and the good that exists in everyone. Monique continually thought, "What would Jesus do?" She was an imitator of Christ. There was no need to wear a bracelet to remind her to handle life's situations the way that Jesus would have handled them; it was her way of life.

The Word of Christ tells us to love others as we love ourselves. This concept came easily to Monique. Even as a small child, she would put others first. She always wanted the best for them, disregarding her own needs and desires. She even placed my feelings and needs above her own.

Money was not an easy subject to talk about, especially to a teenager. At times, we could not afford all of the things that everybody else had. In fact, Monique often seemed to be the one who had the least. But she was grateful for what she had, and if doing without bothered her, she never made it known.

While in high school, one of her favorite teachers had a birthday. Monique wanted to take him a cake. I told her she should have told me earlier, since it was already 9:30 p.m., and I was getting ready to retire for the night. She said it was okay, and I went to bed. I kept hearing noises, so I got up to see what it was and found Monique baking a cake. She looked up at me and said," I found a box of cake mix in the cabinet." We stayed up together until the cake was finished. It is said that hindsight is 20/20. Honestly, I haven't really reflected too much on memories like this until Monique went home to be with the Lord. These times that may have been over-looked before now stand out boldly, demonstrating how much Monique cared for people. She sacrificed for others in small ways but also in very large ways, never asking for anything in return.

When Monique was new in her walk with God, she bonded with one of the girls from her youth. At the time, this girl was older than Monique but just as Monique needed the guidance of an older youth, this person needed Monique's gentle spirit in her life. As the years passed, the friendship drifted, as many relationships do. During that time, my daughter grew very disappointed, as their time together became less frequent. She had thought that this would be a friendship that would last a life-time. However, one day Monique came to me and asked if I would take her to buy a cake and balloons for this person because it was her birthday.

Monique had called her friend's husband and some mutual friends to plan a surprise party. I was shocked, seeing that their relationship was no longer close. In fact, my daughter had shared with me how she felt a little hurt and betrayed by a situation that had occurred in their relationship. I took Monique to the store to purchase cake, ice cream, and balloons. Then I dropped her off at the house; the keys were left under the doormat. It turned out that the night was a great success, and her friend was really surprised that Monique would do this for her, knowing that they were not as close as they had been. Even though she was so young, our daughter was able to put things aside and follow her heart. She fully demonstrated maturity, faithfulness, and love for others, gaining her happiness from knowing there was something she could contribute in making others happy.

Monique sang for the high school of performing arts. Although young, she knew her God-given gifts and abilities. Monique enjoyed singing for her school, but more importantly, it was a platform for her to share God's love. As part of the Youth Praise and Worship Team, Monique was able to reach out to many teenagers, not only to share God's love but to be used as a vessel for God to show teenagers that they could have a life of fulfillment in Christ.

We attend a church that has a three-part mission statement. The third part reads "Advancing the Kingdom of God, first through our circles of influence, and then to nations abroad." Monique had many friends and acquaintances, and in a very gentle and natural way, she advanced the Kingdom of God. I never realized the extent of her influence and her impact on others, nor the level that God had used her to further his kingdom.

Monique knew many people, but she would say that she felt like she did not fit in. She could not find her rightful place. She loved all her friends and acquaintances. I often wondered why she felt that way. The realization came to me one day, not long after our daughter went home to be with the Lord. Monique is in Heaven, a place where she fits perfectly. She is in the presence of the Lord, where her heart's desire has been fulfilled. Monique has found her place, where there is no sickness, evil, or sadness. She exists now in a place of joy and complete perfection.

Since Monique has gone home to be with the Lord, so many of her friends, both teens and adults, have come to me and blessed my life by sharing stories or testimony of their relationship with her. Often, they would tell me about something she did for them—a prayer she said, or a word of encouragement, kindly spoken. Monique was a servant in every way, and I am blessed to call her my daughter. I am grateful for the fifteen glorious years we spent together and all of memories that will last a life time.

There are times when I miss her so deeply my heart aches for her. I think of our hopes and dreams, never to be realized, especially her wedding day. I always use to dream about what it would be like when she chose a wedding dress. I knew it would be beautiful, and I had dreams of seeing her walk down the aisle to get married. Each time I had this thought, God would remind me of Isaiah 61:10: "I will greatly rejoice in the Lord, my soul shall be joyful in my God; for he has clothed me with the garments of salvation, he has covered me with the robe of righteousness, as a bridegroom decks himself with ornaments, and as a bride adorns herself with her jewels." It reminded me that no wedding dress could compare to the robe of righteousness that she now wears in Heaven. I know when she was greeted at the gates of Heaven, she was where she belonged and so longed to be. Monique is home with her Heavenly Father, completely healed emotionally and physically. I know every time she sang in the youth group, she felt that she was in God's presence. Now she truly is praising and worshiping in the presence of Almighty God.

Monique,

Your spirit is alive in me today. I live my life through your legacy. I know that our time apart is short, and that you will be there to greet me when I am called home. I find great peace in knowing that this time will pass ever so quickly, and that we will again be reunited to dwell in Heavenly mansions and to walk together, hand-in-hand, on streets of gold.

Mom

Chapter Two

A Born Leader, Still Teaching

"I tell you the truth, unless you change and become like little children, you will never enter the kingdom of heaven. Therefore, whoever humbles himself like this child is the greatest in the kingdom of heaven. And whoever welcomes a little child like this in my name welcomes me."

—<u>Matthew 18:3-5</u> NIV

Jesus calls us to believe with a child-like faith, accepting Him without question, so that we may enter the Kingdom of Heaven. He gave a perfect example of this through Monique. She never questioned her faith, even when she realized that she would soon be departing from her family and loved ones to rejoin her Heavenly Father. In her innocence, she was capable of passing this blessing along to others, influencing their thinking and opening their eyes to the tremendous possibilities God offers each of us.

She lived her life as a shining beacon of hope, trust, and unswerving faith, sending a message to anyone who met her—a message that helped to open their eyes. One friend now leads a productive life—one that might not have been possible had he not accepted her invitation to 'listen to music.' Even her teachers learned from their student. For one so young, Monique was capable of teaching some of life's most important lessons.

But Monique did not stand upon a soapbox and preach. She did not have to. Monique taught by example and through sharing the marvelous gifts the Lord had given her. It is a lesson many of us need to learn. "Trust in the Lord forever. For in God the Lord, we have an everlasting Rock." (Isaiah 25:4)

She changed my life

I knew Monique only a short while. In that time, she played a huge role in changing my views of the world, which I honestly didn't care about. I destroyed property, played with matches, didn't worry about school, and most of all, I didn't care about God.

I went to her youth group one night because she asked me to go with her. She was sweet and a great girl. I didn't want to say no. Besides, it might be fun listening to music. That night was so much fun. They spoke about God and some of his teachings. They incorporated verses in a way that a youth would understand. I thought that night was so cool that I went to the next youth group night. I met a few people, some of whom I still write to. To make a long story short, I wouldn't be an advanced electronics tech, serving in the armed forces today, if it were not for the life-changing personality and compassion of Monique.

I think about her often, and I will continue to do so till the day I can hear her sing again.

Urban, USN

In Retrospect

I was blessed with the privilege of knowing Monique. She was her own person, and she thought for herself. That's saying a lot, compared to other high school kids our age. She knew who she was. Her confidence and beauty was so inspiring. I was in a choir with her called *Ladies in Harmony*.

We went on a trip to Disneyland as a choir and were told to stay in groups of three or more. Our group consisted of Monique, two other girls, and me. She was such a sweetheart. She almost started to cry when we tried to encourage her to go on the Indiana Jones ride with us. I felt bad, but admired that innocence in her. She must have thought we were going to force her on the ride. We told her she could wait at the exit for us if she felt more comfortable, but she had her own plans for everything.

She wandered away by herself. The other two girls and I just looked at each other, worried because we had lost sight of her and didn't like the thought of her walking around the theme park alone. Whenever we ran into other girls from the choir, we'd ask if they had seen her walking by herself, but no one had. I wasn't too worried. I knew she was a smart girl, and she'd always find her way through anything. About 45 minutes later, we saw her with our teacher. I let out a breath of relief. I was glad to see her smiling and to know she was alright.

I remember in class, she would talk about her church and tell me how much fun it was. I told her I used to go to church when I was a little girl. She said I should go with her. I told her I would. Now I'll always regret never going through with it.

The following year of school I didn't have a class with her and only saw her when we would walk by one another during passing period. Sometimes we would exchange a smile, or a wave, or say a quick hello. I was being a dumb high school kid by not making more of an effort to talk to her or keep in touch.

I really beat myself up about it. In high school if you stop talking to someone, you let things get awkward by acting like you don't know that person anymore, just because you don't see each other every day or talk to them all the time. I see how ridiculous that is now. I know passing period is short, but a quick "how are you" wouldn't have taken too much time. I wish I'd had a hundred awkward "how have you been" conversations with her that year, but instead I chose to be a child about it and be like everyone else, thinking that everyone lives forever. I had no idea that the reason I wasn't seeing her pass by anymore was because she was in the hospital.

I'll never take anything or anyone for granted, ever again. I'll never hesitate to say hello to someone I once knew, or even a happy-looking stranger. What can it hurt? From that experience, I learned that I can regret more of what I don't do than what I actually do wrong. She taught me so much without trying or even knowing she was teaching. I think that's why God took her from us, because she was an angel already. He just didn't want her somehow later on to be tainted by the evils of the world. She was pure and deserved a better place than this. I know she is happy. And I feel very grateful to have known her.

Felicia

For Monique Perez

How do we reason with loss? How do we shelter naïve, unsuspecting joy from the assured gaze of irreconcilable death? For thirty-six weeks I breathed her exchanges of intellect, spirit, and strife. Around my orb of chaos, she was calm and still. In one glance, we affirmed her soul was older than mine. How do I fill the space she left behind? A guru and his disciples are interchangeable. While I gave lessons of cultural literacy, Monique tutored me in clarity, patience, and grace. At fifteen, Monique reminded me to breathe. In a glance, she could encourage me to count to ten instead of yell, steam, or punish. When we truly learn, we must recognize our teacher. I had the pleasure of this mutual privilege.

Having the faith, I do in the current, the tide, the seasons of pain, reckoning, and finding the forgiveness of God, I have come to believe that we have not kept her a second too long in this realm of reasonless living. The wisest souls need not remain, for all has been learned, and they are destined to guide.

It would be an honor to have my path lit by the angel of Monique Perez. For life is not measured by days, months, or years but by the circle of ripples left behind, echoing through the waters of absence.

Allison 2004

Born To Lead

I haven't always been the type of person to go to church as much as I would have had the time for. For some reason, when I met Monique, this changed. Maybe it was because of the fact that she brought it all so meaningfully to me and made me see everything in a different way. I always loved those Wednesdays my friends and I would spend with her at church just seeing her each time on stage, singing with her beautiful, one-of-a-kind smile making life so worthwhile. Ever since she invited me to her church, I have had a craving to go to church and open up to God.

Monique brought so much happiness to my life. She was a great friend. Her spirit was beautiful. Now that I don't get to roam the hallways at school and see her, it brings an awful pain to my heart, which is quickly healed when I remember how much love for God she had, and that now she is definitely in a better place, watching out for everyone she cared for.

One thing happened tonight I will never forget. I went to church again after maybe a year of not attending. I was shocked when I heard that the song, we were about to sing was one she used to sing so beautifully and claimed was her favorite. When we sang it, I felt like she was right there with me, happy and proud that I had gone to church. Monique is someone I will never forget, someone that I will always remember as a leader, leading others to better lives and bringing sense to so many. And for that, I love her.

Martha

Moments like These

I just wanted to say, I love you. Your birthday was a little different this year. I recall you said once that "time goes by, people change, and some of the greatest friends you have can become like strangers." That was the day you spilled your fruit punch all over our bags on the bus on the way back from a Silhouettes performance. I thought, only you could do something like that, making me laugh so hard. It is moments like these that I miss. They were so sincere. At other times, I just look back, and then turn forward again, because you always told me that life moves on . . . ♥ ♥

Unknown

Not by Blood . . . By Heart

Lydia and I would like to thank you for coming. Your love and support during this difficult time means more to our family that we can begin to express.

I am here, today, as a father to ask you not to grieve for Monique, but to celebrate her life—to celebrate fifteen years of life, love, and happiness. When Lydia told me I was going to speak today, she gave me two options. Option one was that I was going to speak. Option two was I was going to speak. When I came into this family, God blessed me with an awesome wife and four kids. Jacob is athletic. Nathan is active in sports, but academic. Bianca is athletic, yet has the ability to entertain. Then there was Monique. I use to tell Monique that she was the coolest chick in the whole world.

I found out quickly, though, that I was not prepared for this large family. I didn't know how to do this. I had to learn to be not only a godly father, but also a godly husband. There were ups and downs, and a few really big bumps in the road. Yet, we always found a way to get through them. During the past three years, something escaped and passed right by me. I completely missed the grace that God had so freely gifted to Monique. What I failed to see was that she had the ability to influence people, large groups of people, by the presence of God in her life.

At Chula Vista High School, Monique was a member of The School of Performing Arts, and a member of the vocal group "The Silhouettes." I saw her make an impact on the entire high school, students and staff included. During Monique's time at Children's Hospital, I witnessed her change the lives of every nurse and doctor that came to know her. Monique not only changed the lives of the youth at church, she changed the church. Most of all, Monique, you have changed me. You changed my heart and showed me how to be a father. Thank you for teaching me that a dad has to be a dad for all seasons. Thanks to you, I now realize that a father takes the good times, but a dad is also a dad during times of hardship.

This past month has been a time of hardship that I cannot begin to express to you. When Monique was admitted to the hospital, I promised her that we would never leave her side. Lydia spent day and night with her. The moments I spent at her bedside was when hospital staff hurt her—the IV's, spinal taps, bone marrow aspirations, and the chemo. I was by her side when Monique passed and went home to God. I am so blessed to have been given three wonderful years, not only to know Monique, but to love her. Monique was not my daughter by blood, but Monique was my daughter by heart.

God revealed to me how much I loved her, and that the love I felt for Monique could not be expressed in words. I am so grateful that I was able to share these revelations of love to Monique. We often become so busy in our daily lives that we miss the blessings God has for us. Before Lydia and I were married, Monique and I had one of many private talks, sitting on her bedroom floor with my back against her closet door. I told her that I could never be her dad, nor would I try. But I loved her as if she were my own daughter.

Many times, I wished that Monique would call me, "Dad." She blessed me with that title possibly three times over the past three years—or so I believed. I recall how much it touched my heart to hear that three-letter word . . . DAD. Recently, I was going through some cards and letters that Monique had written to me, and I found a number of instances in which she had called me, "Dad," several times.

I realized how blessed I was and that all along, she had given me what my heart had desired. But through my own fault, I had missed some of the blessings God had intended for me. So, to all fathers, I encourage you to spend quality time with your children. They are special and deserve our time, devotion, and love. Love them like there is no tomorrow. There may not be. Our children are only loaned to us. They are ours for a season before we all return to God.

Bill Maeda

Servant of the Lord

I'll never forget her angel-like face and bearing. She was a light shining wherever she went. She lit up my Sunday school classes when she came in to see if she could do anything to help, and help she did, just by her presence. The children responded to her and seemed comforted and secure, at peace with her. I can't speak Spanish and that was truly great. Because of her loving, quiet ways, she was alert to the purpose of the lesson and flowed with me. Truly, anyone would know God's Holy Spirit was present in her and through her.

When the Lord took her early, I was saddened, as was everyone. We lost a shining light from God. May we all see her again someday in Heaven? She was a precious gift from above, and we are thankful for her. How wonderful to know she is with the Lord. Thank you, Lord, for the time she spent with us! My memories of Monique are of wonder at her purity, sweetness, love, and Holy Spirit's embedded presence. Thank you, Lord God and Father, for the goodness she has imparted to our lives.

Meredith Campbell

Blowing Bubbles

I played with bubbles today, something I haven't done in years. My friend thought it would be a good idea to blow bubbles in honor of Monique and dedicate them to her. At first, I didn't understand how something as simple as bubbles could honor someone. Now I know that this is yet another lesson that I'm learning from her. Monique did whatever made her happy and brought joy into her life. She never wasted a day. I admire the fact that she can say that she has fulfilled the purpose that God gave her, and I know that she has brought joy to the angels above. Through her death, I am reminded that each day is a gift and that regrets are useless and waste our precious time. I wish to thank Monique for teaching me this, and for showing me how I can allow the Holy Spirit to flow through me and touch all that I meet. I will remember to laugh and play like you have, Monique, and I will blow bubbles.

Unknown

Chapter Three

Wise Beyond Her Years

*"The wise in heart are called
discerning, and pleasant words promote
instruction."*

Proverbs 16:21NIV

How often have the words, "Out of the mouth of babes," been spoken in your hearing? It is a saying that seems to fit Monique. She did not come to know our Lord until the age of ten, but in the five short years that remained of her life, she was like a sponge, soaking up His love and compassion as much as she could. God had a purpose for her. She was His little angel sent to earth to spread His love and encouragement with the sweetness she shared with all she came in contact with.

The words of the wise heard in quietness are better than the shouting of a ruler among fools. (Ecclesiastes 9:17). This Scripture seems to apply to Monique. Who would expect a child of such tender years to know and love the Lord as strongly as she? But Monique did not covet God's love and compassion only for herself. She shared it with everyone who came into her sphere of influence, bringing wisdom and passion that are difficult to find among many adults.

When reading the following stories from family and friends, people who did not have the opportunity to meet Monique may be tempted to remark that she sounds too good to be true. Yet if we believe in Jesus and His promises, we know that angels do exist. In Hebrews 13:2, we are told, "Do not neglect to show hospitality to strangers, for by this some have entertained angels without knowing it." Is it so difficult, then, to believe that Monique was indeed an angel sent to teach those she touched with the meaning of faith, hope, and love? The greatest of these being love.

Reflections of a Friend

I met Monique when she was still a little girl. I remember her because she was always the quiet one, not quiet in the sense that she never said anything, but quiet in that she had something that she wanted to share with you, but was waiting for the right time to say it.

Her smile was so big and charming that she never really had to say 'hi' because once she smiled at you; it was like a big "welcome" sign. Even though she was quiet, people were attracted to her. She had many, many friends. Monique was like a magnet for people who needed help, and she would always have an open ear to help someone with the difficulties of life. She had the kind of personality that we all wish we had—always said the right thing, was there at the right time, put others before herself, and acted unselfishly when a situation seemed impossible.

Monique truly lived a life that most of us could only dream of. Imagine living totally dedicated to helping others, making other people happy, putting her desires on hold so that others could realize theirs. I know that deep down inside that is what we all dream of doing, but so few of us ever take it as far as Monique did. I know that is why most people will never make as big an impact as Monique made in the lives of others.

I remember the day of Monique's viewing. The room was full with standing room only. I thought, "I knew Monique was different, but how could one life make such a difference in the lives of so many?" I didn't know the half of it. The next day at her funeral, there were so many people, a majority of them could not get into the room. It was a fire hazard. Three times as many people were crowding around the doors, waiting to get in. Just the thought that one person could affect so many challenged me to do more, go higher, and be a better person.

I was able to say a few words about Monique at her funeral service. I thought long and hard beforehand about what I wanted to say. The one thing that kept coming into my head was "wisdom." It's true that when someone as young as Monique, who was still a child, got the priorities of life straight, it took wisdom. How else can you explain how much she affected her friends, her school, and her city? Wisdom Monique was wisdom.

My friend Monique changed me almost as much in her death as she did in her life. She only lived fifteen years, but those fifteen years were lived like fifty. It's rare when you get to have a friend like Monique. You cherish every moment with her. Everyone considered her their best friend and wanted time with her. When you look at a life like Monique's, it makes you ask yourself, "Why are we here on earth?" Is it just so we can gain a few memories and experiences, work thirty years at a job, and grow old? I don't think so.

It's so we can make an impact, a difference, and change the world we live in. It's to bring color to a black and white world and to help others when they need it the most. Ultimately, those are the things that make living worthwhile. When we're all on our death bed, we won't be saying, "I wish I would have worked some more overtime," or "I wish I would have bought stock in Google." What we will be saying are things like "I should have spent more time with my kids," "I should have taken my wife out for dinner more often," and "I should have made amends with that family member, it really wasn't that big of a deal." Life is about relationships, building-up other people and bringing out the best in them. Life is about leaving negative things in the past, forgetting the failures of others, and not pointing out their faults.

My friend, I miss you, and thank you for living a true life instead of a fake one. You never tried to please the world to make it look upon you favorably, or twist your belief system to become popular. You gave us an example to follow and strive after. You showed us that even though the path might be difficult, it is possible to do the right thing. I know that you derived your strength from your unwavering belief in God and His Son, Jesus Christ, and it has challenged me to be more like Him.

Life has a way of dragging you down, causing you to forget what living is all about and using up all of your energy on the things that everyone will forget, so that you have no energy to do the things that everyone will remember. Life and death could not drag down my friend Monique. She had something others did not. She really knew in her heart that this world is just a temporary holding place and a dress rehearsal for our life to come. That was her secret. It was a secret she wasn't able to keep inside—made evident by the number of lives she changed.

My friend Monique, it's hard to say goodbye. So, I won't. I'll see you soon enough in the blink of an eye . . . Hi, Monique, gimme a hug!

Eddie

Memories of Monique

As I begin to remind myself of all the great memories of Monique, I get a little choked up. I met Monique when she was just eleven-years-old. I remember a very mature, young girl, who was her mother's "right hand man," so to speak. She had a calm that you don't normally see in young girls her age. As the years passed, I saw a young girl turn into a young lady.

I remember once when we were at church, we started to worship God, and our fingers kept on touching, and from the edge of our eyes, we began to laugh. Her love for God amazed me. Her passion for Jesus was one of those traits that shone. Her faith never wavered, not even for a second. She definitely was a God chaser with a spirit that ran free and proud for her Lord. Monique could encourage us even in the worse circumstances.

For instance, our family had to endure a very painful situation with our youngest child, Madison, in 2003. Even though I loved Jesus, I felt alone and abandoned. I never thought that as a mother, I would come to a point in my life where I would question God about anything. But I did. On April 9, 2003, Monique prayed diligently in a circle with her family and mine about our circumstances. She was a warrior that evening and definitely stopped the devil in his tracks. No matter how she felt, you never would have known that a thirteen-year-old child was praying for my baby. I love that memory because the tables turned in an instant. Peace began to surpass all understanding that day. I will thank Monique for her fortitude and faith always. She showed my husband, and I what Ephesians 6:10 looks like with eyes wide open—"The Armor of God."

Another memory that makes me laugh is when Monique was getting ready for her junior high prom dance. I came by to visit one afternoon, and she asked me if I wanted to see her dress. Of course, I said 'yes.' When Monique came out of her room and into the living room, I could not believe my eyes! Here was a beautiful young lady in a black and white "*I Love Lucy*" dress. Lo and behold, what do my eyes see on her feet . . . her old worn-out black and white converse shoes with everyone's signature or doodling—I can't quite remember, and pony tails on the top of her head. WOW! Monique said to me, "Don't I look awesome?"

Her smile alone made me smile. I replied, "Very pretty dress, but Monique are you really going to wear those shoes?" We both giggled, and she looked at me as if

I were insane. I should have known those shoes were her signature. This memory will last forever. Today, I find myself settled because I know exactly where she is and whom she is with. She is, I'm sure, the same Monique in Heaven looking down upon us, watching over us daily.

She lived life to the fullest and that makes me so happy to have been given the gift of knowing her and her family as we do. Monique is present in my children. I see her in my oldest daughter, who looked-up to Monique in her pre-teen years and still does. I am reminded of Monique when my daughter comes down the stairs dressed in God knows what! Hee, hee, hee! I also see Monique in my youngest daughter. When she plays with her toys, especially her dolls—all of the dolls are named Monique. She takes time and pride in her toys named Monique as if they were jewels of some sort. To this day, my daughter tells me that Monique is dancing with Jesus and the angels in Heaven.

As for me, I experience Monique when the wind blows through the trees, and leaves fall to the ground. I see her in the laughter and smiles of my children while being reminded of something Monique did or stood for. I envision her singing and dancing when I hear one of her favorite songs of praise and worship.

Monique has shown my family and me the reality of Jesus. She faithfully lived her life on earth with integrity and love. She always took time out of her day to witness God's love and peace to someone in need. It's as if she had wisdom beyond her years and really had God's heart in mind. I know that my family is blessed to have had the awesome opportunity to know this beautiful soul.

Monique lives on forever in our lives. She will never be forgotten.

April

Chocolate Cake

I met Monique when she was in the sixth grade. She was very nice and always seemed happy. I remember once on her birthday, I decided to make her a chocolate cake.

Monique had told me that chocolate was her favorite. We had so much fun, even though we didn't really get to eat the cake. We smashed her face in it! She was such a good sport and laughed about it.

One day, she invited me to church. I went with her and her family and had a really good time. On the way home in the car, Monique looked at me and said, "Are you ready for the end?" I just stared at her. I could tell by the tone of her voice that this was a serious question. I did not really give her an answer. You see, she made me really nervous. She said the end will come, and you should know that you are ready. That statement has stayed with me for many years.

When I found out that Monique had gone home to Heaven, I couldn't believe it. I had a track meet the next day, and I dedicated my efforts to her. One thing I can say is that the very question she asked me, I asked about her. I know she was ready, and I know she is in Heaven.

Edgar

Personal Relationship with God

We started attending church in 1998, and instantly welcomed our relationship with Jesus. At the time, I was a single mom. Monique was ten, Jacob was eight, and Bianca four. From the start, we were open to what God had for us. I found what I had been searching for, which was peace. The kids realized it as well. From the beginning, Monique grabbed hold of Jesus and never let go.

I remember one Sunday, Pastor had an altar call. My eyes were closed when suddenly, I felt someone trying to get past me. I opened my eyes and saw Monique walking up to the altar. I started crying. It was a good feeling to know she could hear God's voice and be moved by His spirit. But I also had questioned, why is she going? Is something wrong? Why didn't she tell me?

When we left church, we went to lunch. I questioned her, wondering why she went. Her answer was that she felt led. I asked her why she couldn't tell me. I even asked her if she was mad at me. She said, "No, I just felt the need to go." It seemed as though Monique was hiding something from me. Monique had always been open, and I wondered what was changing. Why couldn't she tell me? A few days later, I spoke to a friend about what had happened. She wondered why I was so concerned. Did it matter? She asked me, "Isn't it enough that you brought her to church to have a personal relationship with God?" She told me to trust God the way Monique did.

I realized that as a mom, I saw her as a little girl and I had to be there to meet her every need. If she needed help, she should come to me. I wasn't seeing her spiritual level or her intimate relationship with God.

Mom

I Love You without Words

I first met Monique at our church youth group when she was ten years old. She was a cute little girl, and I remember she acted older. Somehow, I was drawn to her. At the end of the service, the Pastor asked if there was anyone who wanted to be prayed for. Monique came up, and that was the beginning of many prayer times that I would have with her. That particular night, she said she was dealing with some stuff in her life that she felt she couldn't control, and it hurt her. After we prayed and talked, I felt compelled to give her my promise ring, which meant I would serve God all the days of my life.

I told her I would only give her the ring if she made a promise to God and me that she would do the same. She promised, and I put it on her little finger. I wasn't sure it would fit, but it fit perfectly on her wedding ring finger. From that night, it was a connection that no matter how many times we would get upset or hurt by each other, we would always have our friendship.

I could write a lot of stories about Monique Perez, but this story means the most to me. Not only because she kept her promise, but because, despite all the hurt she had endured physically and emotionally, she still chased God to the end of the race. She made it to the finish line where God was able to tell her, "Well done, my good and faithful servant. Enter into the joy of the Lord." I didn't know that Tuesday, April 26th, would be the last time I would see her.

Monique and I had a look that even if we didn't say, "I love you," the look meant it.

Right before I left, she decided that she wanted a soda. We all walked together, and I was going to say goodbye. I couldn't. When my husband asked me if I had said goodbye, all I could do was look at her and say 'I love you' with my eyes. Then it was over. I relive that moment almost every day of my life and sometimes wish that I would have hugged her and told her I loved her. But then, I remember her face when I was leaving and how she returned that same look. I know it was the best decision I could have made.

Danielle

She Modeled the Message

I will always remember Monique as an example of the way I would hope to be remembered. I first met Monique as a child, working in the nursery at the church we attended. Then, next thing I knew, she was in the youth group, and I thought she was too young. But it seemed to work. It was like she belonged there. She was the kind of girl that you just seemed to love, and you could be assured that you were loved by her. No matter where she went, she always seemed to make a new friend. I think it was easy for Monique because she always gave from her heart.

In retrospect, it is easy to give of your heart when it is a normal natural thing to do. That's the key; giving her heart was just the way she was. It wasn't something she tried to do. It was the kind of person she was. It is easy to love people when you see them through God's eyes, which is exactly what she did. She cared for the lonely, and she was always available to help those who were hurting. Most of all, Monique displayed a Christ-like character. I will always look at Monique as a model—someone I could model my life after. She displayed the qualities of Christ that I hope I will be able to do one day as well as she did.

Mallory

Little Sister

What can I say about my little sister? I didn't really get to know her right from the start. We had different mothers you see, and there was yet another mother and two siblings between us. But when she was the ripe old age of eleven, she came to visit me in El Paso, Texas, one summer. I always thought she was so cute. When I first saw her that summer, I remember thinking that she reminded me of someone. I couldn't tell who.

As the days went by and we talked, I started to realize who she reminded me of. We were driving to Wal-Mart one afternoon, and she was really quiet. I asked her if she felt sick, or if she was home sick. She responded with a weak 'no.' I asked what was wrong. "Are you bored?" But she said, "No." Just then she asked me if I had ever gotten used to my parents being divorced. I looked at her and the look in her eyes was wise beyond her years with a hint of pain. It was at that moment that Monique became "Mini me." I talked to her and told her that I had never gotten used to my parents' divorce. She said, me, too. I joked with her and said that now my parents cannot get together because if mine do, yours won't.

We both laughed. We talked for about an hour-and-a-half outside of Wal-Mart. Monique told me how she believed in God, and how she got her strength from God. Our connection was through Christ Our Savior. I miss her so much, especially as I write this. I feel as if I just opened my heart, and I'm feeling the sorrow of not watching her grow up in my life. Monique also prepared me for the day that I would have to say goodbye to her. I'm telling you, she was wise beyond her years! The story goes like this. .

That same year that she came to visit me, I was going through a very difficult time with my son, Michael. Michael had left home, and I did not know where he was. He was fifteen years old, and I was terrified. I kept in touch with Monique through the Internet. One day, we were instant messaging each other, and she asked how I was doing. I told her about Michael running away, and that I was so scared for him. She then asked me, "What are you scared about?" I told her I was scared of getting a phone call and someone telling me that he was dead. She replied, "Why are you scared of that?" Then the words that I now live by came on the screen— ***"It's only when you die that you begin to live."***

I believe now that Monique was a messenger of our Lord, and that she touched many people and brought them to Christ. I believe it was her mission that in her short lifetime she accomplished what most of us can't. She was destined to do what she did. She did it with all the grace and the beauty of the One above. He called her to His side because her work here on earth was done.

In His Name,

Linda Barrio

Chapter Four

Praising God

***"Hear this, you kings! Listen, you rulers! I
will sing to the Lord, I will sing;
I will make music to the Lord, the God of
Israel."***
—Judges 5:3 NIV

Whenever people sing spiritual songs and praises to God, they are worshiping and adoring Him twice as much as they do with the spoken word. Song is twice prayer. It is a wonderful way to show our Lord how much you love Him. As young as she was, Monique seemed to understand this. The Lord had blessed her with a beautiful singing voice, and she never failed to return His gift by using it to worship Him and inspire others around her with the desire to worship God.

Many people have probably heard the term, 'babe magnet.' Well, Monique was a 'God magnet.' Wherever she went, people could not help being drawn to her and through her to the Lord. Her love for Our Savior shone like a mighty beacon, drawing all who gazed upon her, enticing them to sing and dance their praises to God. The Lord must have smiled fondly as he observed Monique from His Heavenly throne. He knew that He had created the perfect child, a child who would bring many into His loving embrace.

Monique was the ideal answer to the question: "What can I do? I am only one person." She proved to everyone she came into contact with that one person can make a difference. And if an individual is capable of changing the lives of many, can the rest of the world be far behind? Monique is an example we should all follow. How marvelous it would be if we could teach everyone to sing and praise the Lord as Monique did. The joy that followed would soon drive evil and darkness away forever. "Therefore, I will give thanks to You, O Lord, among the nations. And I will sing praises to your name." (Samuel 22:50).

Left Behind

When I remember Monique, the one thing that stands out most is her love for worshiping Jesus. She was young, but had a great love for the Lord. I remember the times when she would stay home on a Friday night to lead our women's group in worship. When most teens were going out with their friends, Monique would gladly stay back and wholeheartedly lead full-grown woman in worshipping our Lord. It was so beautiful and awesome for her age.

I remember standing behind her during our Sunday services, being blessed by her focus and heart for the Lord. At an age when most teens are so aware of "themselves" and trying to be "cool," Monique didn't seem to care what others thought. She just loved being in the Lord's presence with His people. What an awesome testimony she left behind. I believe she touched more people with the love of God than most of us do in the greater number of years we have here on earth. I know you're praising Him up there and dancing before Him unhindered!

Vicky

Loving Everyone

I remember Monique always made me feel like I was a part of her family. She called me "tia," which means 'aunt.' She would come up to me with her big smile, give me a hug and say "Hi, tia." One time, Lydia and I went to Jerome's Furniture Store. I was looking for furniture for my new apartment. I remember my daughter Annie and Monique playing like little girls in the bedroom furniture section pretending that it was their bedroom. It was fun to be around Monique. She had a way of making people feel special, regardless of who they were.

I remember she always wanted everyone to get together for picnics or barbeques at her house. She loved people, young or old. They were special to her. I guess it was because everyone is special and important to God, so it became important to Monique because she loved God! Her love for the Lord could be seen. It was not just words. Her actions revealed her love for God by the way she treated people. What I miss most is watching Monique sing to God during praise and worship at church. It always caught my attention and amazed me to see such a young person pour out their heart to God the way she did. I look forward to being with her in Heaven someday, praising God together, face to face with our Savior.

Tia Sofia

Beautiful Inside and Out

There is so much to say about Monique Perez. She was the most beautiful person inside and out. She inspired everyone she knew, including me. Monique taught me to not take things for granted, such as life, friends, church, everything. I remember all the memorable times Monique and I spent together. They were always happy ones.

My most memorable memory with her was when we went to a big Fourth of July crusade. There were several Christian bands. One was Audio Adrenaline. That band started singing one of their songs called "Hands and Feet." Monique and I ran to the big crowd that was jumping up and down. We had so much fun together. I guess I could say we jumped like we had never jumped before. That's one of the things about Monique. She brought a smile to everyone's face. She was such a joy to be around. One of the physical characteristics I remember about her was her awesome smile and her hair. Now that she has passed, we keep her in our memories. So, I guess we can say: We miss you, Monique Ashley Perez.

Briana

Monique's Love for Music

After Monique passed away, I remember telling her mother that the one thing I regret not ever doing was hearing Monique sing on stage at church. I knew how much she loved the Lord, and how much she loved to praise and worship him, and it saddened me that I never saw it. My consolation is knowing that she is now in Heaven singing praises to her Lord and Savior, and that one day I will join her in that Heavenly choir. Thinking of this, though, made me recall Monique's love for music.

When she was little, she must have had every sing-along video that existed! She used to sing and dance around the house with her brother and cousin. They loved watching Barney all the time, and naturally, they used to sing the Barney theme song, "I love you. You love me. We're a happy family. With a great big hug and a kiss from me to you, won't you say you love me too?" I can still see her beautiful smile and sparkling eyes.

When Monique was eleven, her mother sent her to visit me for a few days. One day, her cousins, Monique, and I were lying around in bed, talking. We leaned over and hugged her and started singing: "You are my sunshine, my only sunshine. You make me happy, when skies are gray. You'll never know dear, how much I love you. Please don't take my sunshine away!" It was so funny! She just laughed at us and thought we were crazy! But now I thank God for those silly memories. She truly was my sunshine, as I'm sure she was for many people.

Stephanie

His Side of the Sky

I would like to say that I am honored and humbled by the words that have been spoken. God really knows what He is doing when he causes paths to cross. I wrote something because Jose had mentioned to me about her 'my space.' So, I kinda wrote something after praying and thinking about it one night. I think of Monique's death and don't know what to say. I mean, who really knows what to say? The truth is, her death leaves no room for words. Ask anyone about her life, and the words will not cease. Those words usually are accompanied by tears or very strong emotions.

When I think of Monique, I see a huge smile and brilliant eyes staring at me. It makes me think of Jeremiah 29:11: "I know the plans I have towards you, plans to give you a hope and a future." Monique did have a hope and a future. You could see that in her eyes. But most of us, in our selfish ways, wanted her future to be with us on this side of Heaven. Monique is now where her future and hope were founded from the beginning. The last time I heard her sing was at a youth conference. The song Monique sang went like this:

"I want to sing; I want to fly. I want to see from your side of the sky."

The song was titled "After the Music Fades." Simply put, she is in the place she sang about long ago. The music has faded. She is singing a song and is on His side of the sky. No one, not a single one of us, will live the same life because she was in our lives. However brief or however long her time was with us is not relevant. What is important today is what did you learn? What did you experience? What did you see? More importantly, what are you going to do about it?

Death is interesting because it causes us to re-evaluate and prioritize what is really of value in our lives. I hope that Monique's life is not taken for granted now that she is no longer with us. What we thought were small pieces of Monique living within us are no longer pieces. What we have inherited from Monique is the Spirit and a love that transcends this world. We have inherited from Monique the ability to enjoy simple things and love without conditions or inhibitions.

J. Keren

You Have Turned

The first time I saw Monique was at church during praise and worship. She had a way of standing out. Monique was the kind of person that you would notice in the middle of a dust storm. She was a diamond, set apart in a world comprised of coal. I believe God was having a really good day when He created Monique.

I was sitting in church by myself. This was pre-stepdad, pre-marriage. I was looking across the church when I spotted this diamond, casting out beams of light everywhere. Not only did I wonder who that was. I thought, what is that? There she was with her hands raised.

This ten-year-old girl was praising God like there was no tomorrow. There was only the moment that she was in, just her and God. Then she started turning and jumping. The next thing you know, people around her began to turn and jump. In retrospect, I am not at all surprised. This is the effect that Monique had on people, no matter where she was or what she was doing. She was a leader, a true revolutionary. People gravitated toward her. She shared the love of God in all that she did. God's love was all that she was. She was able to share this love, and people found it easy to receive.

I often wondered about how she was able to do this. I even found myself gravitating toward her. There was something totally captivating about her. After knowing her for the next few years, I soon came to realize that what you saw was what you got. Nothing fake, nothing put on. She was a hundred percent, the real deal. I think human nature likes honesty. We like knowing what we are going to get. With Monique, you knew you were getting God, and that made it easy to receive Him. Through the love of God in her life, you really could have your mourning turned to dancing, and your darkness turned to light.

Bill Maeda

Chapter Five

A Heart that Inspired and Motivated Others

"But just as you excel in everything—in faith, in speech, in knowledge, in complete earnestness and in your love for us—see that you also excel in this grace of giving."

—2 Corinthians 8:7 NIV

Every person on earth needs a little inspiration from time to time, especially in this day and age when evil seems to run rampant throughout the world. And there is no better type of inspiration than when it is divine. In examining Monique's life, it is clear that her purpose was to inspire everyone who was blessed to come in contact with her. During her brief time on earth, her gentle and loving spirit taught others about God's love, as she lived her life as a shining example of what she shared with others. Monique believed in the Lord so strongly that even during her final days in the hospital, she was more concerned for the sick infants she heard crying than for herself.

For those who never had the chance to have their lives touched by Monique, it may be difficult to believe that a child could be so selfless, loving, and inspiring. Yet, after reading the stories and letters contained in this book, there is little doubt that Monique was a child of God. Monique was a messenger sent to assure us that God is love, and His love encompasses everyone, whether or not we chose to follow His commandments. Monique as an ambassador to Christ demonstrated Faith, Hope and Love and to her last breath demonstrated that the greatest of these was love.

Monique was able to motivate others to try harder and become better people. She was a shining example of a faith so powerful that even death did not frighten or deter her. She stayed true to her belief in God's love and compassion until she was able to join Him once more in Heaven. Monique set an example that we should all strive for.

Revolutionary

There are so many amazing things about Monique. I remember when I first met her. She was in my freshman English class and always said, 'Hi,' to me. I liked that she didn't even know me but she would still speak to me. After a while, we became friends. She actually inspired me to be a better person in life and in Christ. I had a lot of issues with my life, and I was having problems with God. Knowing Monique and her love for Him made me want the same thing. She changed my entire spiritual walk.

I thought it was amazing how someone her age could have such a strong relationship with God, and how open she was about it. She didn't care about what people thought because she knew who she loved was real. That was what really touched me and changed my life. Even now, when I'm having problems and doubt, I just think of her, and I know I can do better, just like her. I hope this helps those who read this, and I pray this book reaches people and makes a difference in their lives, knowing about an angel that lived on earth. God Bless.

Beth

Who I Am Today?

I love Monique more than anything, and I always will. I thank her for who I am today. I am a United States Marine, and Monique played a great part in my success as a Marine. She was my motivation through what was the hardest time of my life. I would not be the better man that I am today without her influence. With Monique in my heart and mind, I know I can find success in anything. I have never been so grateful and always will be, through this life and into eternity.

Tony

Determination

One thing that I'll always remember about Monique is her determination. A favorite and funny memory is of Bianca's birthday party at the apartment when we went swimming. Jake was trying to teach her how to dive but she only did belly flops. As much as it probably hurt her, Monique kept trying because she really wanted to learn. Seeing her so determined inspired me in a way to go after my dreams. No matter how many times I fail—I just keep getting up and trying until I succeed. Whatever Monique did, she always did her best. She was the greatest role model a girl could ever hope for. She was an intelligent, graceful, funny, and caring young lady that will always have a place in my heart. I love her.

Serena

Monique: A Great Influence

Monique was a great influence in my life. I met her in high school where we both sang in the SCPA program at Chula Vista. She always made me smile. I knew if I had a problem, she would be there for me.

I remember one time; I had a big fight with my boyfriend. He broke up with me, and I was very upset. I was crying and could not stop. Monique came over and gave me the biggest hug, and held me until I stopped crying. When I did, she looked at me and said, "Everything is going to be okay." She also said, "He is not worth it, but that if it was meant to be, he will come back." Ultimately, she was right. He was not worth it.

Tiffany

Grown To Admire You

I'm not sure how long Monique and her family had been attending the World Harvest Christian Center. I had seen her a couple times, I hardly talked to her. She must have been eleven years old at the time. I think I smiled at her once in a while. Monique was at the age where she could attend the weekly youth services. It wasn't long before she became a part of our group. Monique must have been the youngest girl in our group for a long time. We didn't mind, and neither did she. I think that's what made her mature faster, since she was always around older people. Sometimes it didn't even seem that way because she had become our age in spirit.

Throughout the last six years of her life, our friendship grew into something more. I can honestly say that she was like a sister to me—someone I felt I could help along those tough teen years. Not only did I help her, she helped me more than I think she realized. Monique was a reminder to me how innocent and new life could be. That's how she lived. To her, everyday was a new day. She never wasted a minute of her time.

One of the things I admired most about Monique was that no matter what anyone said, she loved God with all her heart. No matter what went on at school, she would talk about her church and her relationship with God. That took guts! She put meaning in the word bold. There's rejection, ridicule, persecution, and who knows what else! Of course, these minor obstacles never stopped her. That's why people loved being around her. She was a true follower of Christ through and through.

I think one of the biggest things she taught me was to always say, "I Love you, Mom." I didn't have the best relationship with my mom, for many reasons, but once we became closer, she would always have me say, "I Love You," to my mom before I hung up the phone with her, and anytime I would leave home. It seemed like I was always at her house—in the pool, or walking to the Seven/Eleven Store. I miss those days and I really miss Monique.

I remember when we sang in front of the youth group. Our youth pastor was teaching about love, and we sang a song related to the subject. It was so funny because we had practiced only a couple of days before the performance, so we decided not to sing. At the last minute, our youth pastor wanted us to sing the song. We performed with little practice, but it ended up sounding okay.

Maybe about a year or so afterward, Monique, two girlfriends, and I thought of doing a skit with a song from a youth conference that our youth group had attended earlier that year. We decided to practice at my house. I remember that we kept getting frustrated, and fought once, but Monique was the one that simmered everything down. She always seemed to have a calming influence in the face of a storm.

I remember when Monique went to Prom with Andy Rubalcaba. She was so excited! Can you believe that she actually wanted Andy to take his parents' van to prom? She thought the van was so cool. I went with her to get her nails and hair done. She had me take pictures of her doing her nails and hair. Unfortunately, I couldn't stay for the pictures of them together. However, she told me all about the prom and everything. Her dress was a burgundy/black because she wanted to wear a black dress with small hot-pink polka dots.

About a year later, I went on a mission trip to Romania. I originally had planned to have a handful of girlfriends spend the night at my house the night before I left. But my mom wouldn't allow me to have them over at the last minute. She told me I could choose one. I chose Monique. She was more excited than I was and helped me pack my last few things.

At the airport, my parents were the only ones that could go with me past baggage claim. Monique wouldn't let me cry. She told me, "Don't cry. You have to be strong for your parents. It will tear them up inside if they see that you are scared. Don't cry, don't cry." As I passed through the baggage claim, I looked back and saw Monique with a huge smile, mouthing the words "don't cry." I didn't cry on the plane either. I was so scared of the lift-off, but I all I could hear was my heart saying, "Don't cry, and stay strong."

In August of 2003, our youth group hosted a conference. Monique sang. She already had been singing with the youth band, but she was so excited about this conference. She had so much fun. I was proud of Monique. I was dating a man, and we were starting to get closer. Monique told me that she had a good feeling about it. She was excited for me. I used to tell her that what I felt for him was different than the last relationship I had. Whenever we talked about it, we became giggly.

I loved the relationship Monique and I developed over the years. We both worked in the children's ministry. We would hardly see each other at church. Even though our schedules were different, when we found time to spend with each other, we made it count. We would spill everything that happened during the time we hadn't talked.

I found out Monique was in the hospital on April 11, 2004. I had just come back from a mission trip. That day, five friends and I went to see her in the hospital. It was really hard to go to the hospital to see her. It took at least a half an hour to get there. I only went that one time. It was the only time I was able to tell her I loved her. I could tell right away that Monique was surprised to see us. The first thing I noticed was her face. It was so swollen that I wanted to cry. But I knew that she would feel bad. So, I thought of what she would tell me, "Don't cry, and stay strong." It hurt me to see her that way. However, I knew she was a fighter.

I was at a conference with other members of the youth group in Temecula, California, when she passed away. At the conference, the youth pastor requested everyone to pray for her. I prayed with everything I had. As we went home, I was hoping for the best, but preparing for the worst. When I heard that Monique had passed, I dropped to the floor and started screaming. I couldn't believe it. I thought that I had fallen asleep and was having a nightmare. Then I heard my brother, Andrew, crying as well. He used to have a crush on Monique, but later just thought of her as a close friend. I think I cried myself to sleep. I was heartbroken, and upset with God. I wanted to tell her how much I loved her, and how much she meant to me—how she changed my life. It wasn't fair. At the same time, I felt relieved that she was out of pain and free to be where she ultimately wanted to be, in Heaven.

Sometimes, it's like she's on a long vacation, and I'll see her again someday. Maybe it's not the best way to deal with it, but I can't get over the fact that she's gone. Most days, I don't think about it, and I'm fine. It's those special days that something reminds me of her, and I wish it was different. My spirit is joyful because I know that Heaven is where she longed to be. On the other hand, my soul still mourns her absence.

I can only imagine what it was like. I know that for her to leave her life, she had to have seen Heaven. I know she saw Jesus, and He showed her, what her sacrifice would bring and how her friends would become closer, maybe even closer to Him. She saw what an impact her life had made, and how much more it would be if she sacrificed it. She is a true follower of Christ. She sacrificed everything she knew, family, friends, and life, to be with Jesus. You can't top that one. I have grown to admire her more every day.

Denise

Most Inspirational Silhouette

Thank you for giving us the opportunity to present the Most Inspirational Silhouette Award for 2005. We also would like to thank the students and staff of the School of Creative and Performing Arts. You have made the past year a little more bearable. This award is especially appropriate for us as Monique was and continues to be our inspiration.

While in the ICU at Children's Hospital, rather than be concerned for her own health, Monique's concern was for the babies she could hear crying in the adjacent rooms. This was so like her. She was facing an uphill struggle, but still reached out towards the sick and lost. When I say that Monique is our inspiration, I mean this in the most genuine terms. She has inspired us to live even when we wondered if we could. Most of all, Monique has inspired us by showing us the way to love. For this we will forever be grateful. Now that all has been said and done, we realize that out of a tragic situation, God still finds a way to turn a tragedy into a blessing.

Lydia and Bill Maeda

How Great and Powerful God Is

Today is an awesome day for me because an Angel, a messenger of God, came to me at night in a vision. She use to live on this earth and her name is Monique Perez. Before I continue, let me tell you how my day was, yesterday. I had no strength and felt lifeless and restless because of all of the affairs and trials of life. I was feeling really down and struggling to keep the faith. On the night of May 22, 2006, before I lay to sleep, I was reading Matthew 6:25 where Jesus is commanding us not to worry about anything, that God is Father, and He will feed, provide for us, and tell us how much more valuable we are than birds and the grass of the fields. His word brought life to me.

I fell asleep in God's peace. In my dream, I was worshiping God with my hands lifted toward Heaven. I literally felt as though my hands were in Heaven, Monique by my side. She opened her mouth and her words were like no others. She expressed to me how great and powerful God is. Oh! How I wanted to hear it again. I asked her, "Please say it again! Say it again!" She was so beautiful, filled with the glory of God. She was a spirit in white. Her hair was loose and wavy, and light was all around her.

I continued to worship God while lying there with my hands lifted to Heaven. Then a hand came from nowhere and took me by the hand. I began to say, "Yes Lord! Yes Lord! Take me," but it wasn't time for Him to take me because I had to share this with her beautiful mother and everyone who reads this book about how God is still using Monique to encourage others.

Now, let me tell you about today. This morning, I awoke with so much energy and a desire to pray like I have never prayed before. God's great and wonderful power was backing me up. Monique had expressed to my spirit how great and powerful God is because she had been with the Great and Powerful One, and no one else on this earth could communicate it to me the way she did until they, too, have been with the Great and Powerful, Awesome God! Amen!

I look forward to really understanding how great and powerful God is. Now I only have a glimpse of it, but when I meet Him someday face-to-face, I will understand just as Monique does.

Unknown

Dedicated Season

Monique is my stepsister. I wish I could say that we always got along or that everything between us was perfect, but that isn't quite true. Then again, what brother and sister do always get along? I remember she often wanted to talk to me about God and my relationship with Him. There also were times that she would ask me if I wanted her to pray for me. Of course, I said "no," but there were times when I wish I would have said "yes." There are times now that I would say "yes" . . . if I only could.

I play a goalie for my high school Lacrosse team. The early part of the season was not going that great. We seemed to be finding ways to lose games. My dad suggested that maybe I should dedicate the remainder of the season to Monique. I thought about it, and as I stood in the goal I said, "Win or lose, I dedicate the season to you Monique."

I felt a peace come over me, I could feel her presence. That was the turning point of the season. We started winning games, and the team really improved. I finished the season with 263 saves, which is a school record, and I was named Defensive Player of the year. I know that she was with me every game. I believe that the peace and calm I felt during the game was because I knew she was there. I know she will be with me every game now.

Nathan

Messenger

I have sat for hours thinking about the correct way to write this. Do I write about memories? Do I write about what it is like to have a niece like Monique? Then I thought it would be best if I just told you about Monique, and had to smile. Even after all the time she has been gone, Monique still will be reaching people and telling them about God. Monique was a very special young lady. It is said that God sends friends disguised as angels. To tell you about Monique and her life is very easy. "Bless the Lord, you His angels. Mighty in strength, who performs His word, obeying the voice of His word! (Psalms 103:20).

The Greek word "angelos" means "messenger," and that is exactly what Monique is, a messenger of God—an angel. Angels are purely spiritual beings that do God's will. Monique did exactly that each and every day. Thomas Aquinas believed that angels influence mankind by illuminating one's mind with an idea, and with few words. Monique could and would do this. She did do this to me the last time I saw her over Christmas break at my parents' house. We had gotten together to celebrate Jesus' birth in 2002.

Monique was not interested in playing games or going outside to run and play. She came to me to talk about the Bible and asked which one was my favorite verse. Then she asked why. I could see the interest in her eyes. Over my visit, we talked several times about the Bible, and she just made me think. She "illuminated one's mind with an idea." How I wish I could hold her one last time and give her a kiss, just say "thank you." If I could only hear her one more time answer the phone when I call and say, "Hello Tio."

The life and story of Monique is very inspiring, right up to when she left us to go to God. Some may remember her for how beautiful she was, others how funny, and still others the wisdom she spoke with. As for me, a proud uncle, I can't remember much, but most of what I do remember is the example she was able to set, not only to her sister, brother, and friends, but the example that she was able to set for me.

I remember her as a baby and as she was growing up. Most of all, I remember her setting an example for us right up to her last minute. When I think of Monique, I see her lying there with her arm raised, still praising God. There is no doubt in my mind that Monique heard the phrase, "Well done my good and faithful servant." Love you, Monique. See you again!

Uncle Gilbert

Chapter Six

Always Sharing God's Peace, Love and Joy

*"If you, then, though you are evil, know
how to give good gifts to your children,
how much more will your Father in heaven
give good gifts to those who ask him!"*

—Matthew 7:11 NIV

This Scripture is one that everyone should constantly keep in their minds and hearts. God always gives us the gifts of His love, peace, and joy, which He then wants us to share with others, just as Monique did. But He does not stop there. Many people do not realize the full extent of God's willingness to give. They say, "God is too busy to worry about the day-to-day events in our lives." Or they will tell you, "God won't interfere; that's why we have free choice."

Poor, sad, misguided souls; freedom of choice also means that we can ask Him to interfere. The Bible tells us over and over, "Ask and you shall receive." But you have to believe you will receive it, too. That belief is faith. Sometimes, the gift may come in a different form than one might expect, but the gift will be granted in His time. God also gives gifts we don't ask for. Jesus was a fantastic gift—the greatest one we could ever receive. And to help us along the way, God gives gifts like Monique, who truly must have been an angel visiting from Heaven to teach us how to share God's love, peace, joy, and other gifts like the special talents He gives to each of us.

Children often are selfish, especially when they are young. It is a trait that needs to be gently unlearned. Yet Monique seemed to be born without this natural tendency. She was so filled with God's love that it was as though she would burst at the seams if she didn't share it with all she came into contact with. What a powerful gift all of us could give if we would just choose to share God's love and blessings with others the way that Monique did.

WWJD

Monique had a spirit of love and compassion that was all-consuming. She was a person you always could count on and was the first to say, "Mom, is there anything thing you need?"

I was a single parent for most of Monique's life. I recall a time when she was eight years old. I was sick with the flu, but still had to go to work. As a single parent, I did not have the luxury of missing. I worked for a few hours and finally, my boss sent me home. We didn't have a car at the time, so I had to take the trolley. When I walked through the front door, the kids were so excited to see me. Monique could tell straightaway that I was exhausted.

It was early afternoon, and I remember lying on the couch. When I awoke, the house was dark and silent. I looked at the clock and was surprised that it was 9:30 p.m. I sat up, forgetting where I was, and for that matter, when it was. As I started to rise, I felt someone or something on the floor beside me. Monique was curled up, asleep. I was not sure what had happened. Then Monique awoke, looked at me, and said, "Mom, are you okay?"

I apologized to her for falling asleep. With her calm, reassuring spirit, Monique said, "it's okay, Mom. I heated some soup, and the babysitter fed Jacob. I gave Bianca a bath, changed her diaper, and put her to bed. Monique told Jacob to sleep in Bianca's bed, and that she would stay with me to make sure that I was okay.

Sometimes it seemed as though our roles were reversed. Was I the mom, or was Monique? She always seemed to have the ability to restore and maintain order. I know this is why I relied on her so much, especially when it came to taking care of her brother and sister. She had a natural way of making the kids feel safe and secure. Today, as the kids are growing up, I can see they have become products of not only what Monique did, but more importantly, what they saw her do.

There was a trend a few years ago. Kids were wearing bracelets with the acronym on it "WWJD." This stood for "What Would Jesus Do?" Monique, as a spirit-led teenager, doing exactly as Jesus would do. She humbled herself and placed the needs of others before her own. She was and is a great example, not only to her brother and sister, but to me as her parent.

Mom

In Loving Memory of Monique Perez

There are so many wonderful ways to describe Monique. She was an angel sent to us from God. She always tried her best to impact everyone's life in a positive way. Her beautiful, kind words would comfort everyone around her, even those who didn't know her. She was perfect, everything that anyone would look for in a person. She was beautiful, kind, understanding, full of joy and hope, and she was funny. She's the only person I know who could turn the worst day into the best day you've ever had, just by telling you one of her corny, silly jokes. She will always be in our hearts; as long as we don't forget that we will always be in hers.

Unknown

Sleeping Beauty

I met Monique in seventh grade. I will never forget . . . We were best buddies: Marissa, Christy, Monique, and I. It was a lot of fun with plenty of great memories. The best part was when she took us to church. In the tenth grade for air band, she was Sleeping Beauty, and I was Belle. Everybody was stressed. She was the only one who was calm. She was wonderful that night.

When she got sick, I wrote her a note, telling her what a good person she was, and that she would be okay. I never had a chance to give her that note, but I now know that she knows, and that she is okay, just like I said she would be. I love you, Monique, and I thank you.

Angelica

True Friend

Monique was the one girl who didn't care if she was seen with me. She could be with her friends, and still, she would say 'hi' to me. I do not think she ever noticed how different I was from her other friends. She was a person who was not self-conscious about what their friends would think if she was seen with me. For that care and consideration, and for those moments of unconditional love, I thank her. I love Monique because she was a true friend.

Cynthia

Instant Friends

Monique and I went to the same elementary school. The sad thing is that we didn't have any classes together until seventh grade. Once we got to seventh grade, we were in the same science and health classes. We became friends almost instantly. But then, she instantly became friends with everyone in class. I remember that we liked to talk about school, church, and music.

I want to share a little story. It's not a great story, but it is so Monique. It was Valentine's Day. Monique walked into class with at least five long-stem roses in her hand. In middle school, you can send roses to a person on Valentine's Day. But you would expect to see a person with a rose here or a rose there . . . not five.

Dari J.

Kindness

The thing I remember most about Monique was her kindness to my children. They adored her. Once on a Wednesday night in children's church, she did Courtney's hair, and allowed her to keep some rubber bands as bracelets. You would have thought that Courtney had received a diamond bracelet. She was so excited and happy. She thought Monique was awesome. Kindness is a fruit of the Spirit, and Monique exemplified that in her life.

Christine

Always There

I remember the first time I met Monique in middle school. I was having a real bad time. I had just lost my grandfather and thought that there was no other reason to live. Monique came to me and introduced herself. She asked if she could help in any way, because she had noticed that I looked like I needed a friend. I had never felt so comfortable talking or opening up to someone I had just met. It felt like the right thing to do. It was so hard to talk to anyone else, and I felt like she could help me. So, we talked for a while, and I told her what was going on.

I'm sorry to say it, but I was ready to kill myself. I don't know how to put it any better. Monique talked me out of it. She helped me through everything, and told me that if I ever needed anyone to talk to, if I needed anyone or anything, to let her know, and that I should know that this conversation was not over. After that, whenever we had a chance, we would talk. Monique's promise was good. She was always there and made me feel like I was wanted. She told me that my family, my friends, and even she needed me. She told me that God would take me when we were both ready.

I had never in my life felt so good about life, myself, or everything and everyone around me. I couldn't thank her enough, and I will never stop thanking her. Even though she is gone, I still talk to her, I feel like she still answers me. When I feel that I need her, I look back and think about all the things she used to tell me and all the things she would say and do to help. She was always there and still is. Every day, I think about how lucky everyone was to have Monique in their life.

Nicole

She is Love

When I talk about Monique, it is inevitable that the clichés will come forth. There is of course, her smile and her personality. People would talk about how much fun she was, and how she impacted everyone she met. It would be so refreshing to speak of the real Monique, absent of clichés. If you were lucky enough to have her as a friend, she was as faithful as a friend could be. Words spoken in confidence were honored and never fell into the rumor mill. Monique was the real deal. As a friend, you knew exactly what you were getting. She was highly trustworthy and would put the needs of friends and family before her own. If you needed her she was there, ready and willing to help out or just to listen if an ear was all you needed.

Monique saw people through God's eyes. She never judged others; she just loved. Her perception of the human race was internal. It didn't matter what you were: a punker, rocker, athlete, skater, socialite, or just an average person; she loved you from the inside out. She never tried to be something or someone she wasn't for any reason. She respected everyone for who they were. Monique always found the good that exists in everyone.

Monique had the love of God in her heart, the Holy Spirit in her soul, and the favor of God in her life. She blended with crowds, yet her light shone forth in everything she did, and all that she touched prospered. She understood God and found intimacy with him—the type of intimacy that many of us desire. As her mother, I still experience a great chasm in my life—a chasm so deep that any attempt to fill it would fall woefully short. I find moments of solace in my life as I grow to accept the fact that my daughter, my Sleeping Beauty, my right-hand man, is exactly where she wanted to be, seated in the presence of God Almighty.

Forever missed . . . never forgotten . . . eagerly awaiting our reunion.

Mom

Loved by All

I did not know Monique for long, but in the short time I knew her, I loved her as we all did. She was just one of those people everyone loved. She was the one person I knew I could always go to; I could trust her no matter what.

I remember trying to talk to her across the room in first period English. We would throw makeup back and forth to each other. Monique, Victoria, and I would pass notes and talk about anything and everything in the middle of geometry class as though no one was around. She made things more exciting, fun, and happier.

Then I remember when she wasn't there, and how sad I was when I found out she was ill. When she wasn't in school, we would text message each other. She always would ask how I was, and I would tell her, "Who cares how I am doing? How are you doing?" She never stopped caring about us. I will never stop caring about her. I love you, Monique, and miss you.

Erica

Chapter Seven

The Smile that Lives Forever

**"She is clothed with strength and dignity;
she can laugh at the days to come."
—Proverbs 31:25 NIV**

"Make a joyful noise unto the Lord all ye lands!" Monique certainly did just that. Regardless of what type of day she might have been having, it did not seem to matter. She stood as a shining example of God's love for us even until the day she rejoined our Heavenly Father. Could you face death as easily as Monique—with a smile on your face, still bearing the love and concern for others you had shown for years? There was never a question in her mind that she would be joining the Father in Heaven—no regrets that she would not have another seventy or more years to live on earth.

Monique couldn't wait to see God again. If she truly was an angel sent to earth, it must have been very hard for her to be separated from the Almighty. As much as her family and friends love and miss her, our pain would be small compared to her desire to be with the Lord again. And who could blame her? Although we all long to be in His presence—to spend eternity with Him, we know we must wait for our time. But we cannot remember what it was like before He formed our essence and placed it within our mothers' wombs in preparation for our time here. It would seem that Monique could, and if she truly was an angelic being sent to bring God's people closer to Him, she certainly could have remembered.

She clothed her spirit in strength, kindness, love, and compassion, living as Jesus wants us to live, and following the first two commandments to the best of her ability. She loved God above all others and everyone else as He wants us to love each other. She did not care if you were popular, smart, witty, or beautiful. Her only desire was that you belonged to God and that was good enough for Monique.

Smile: to Look Joyous, to Favor

This defines Monique. Except she didn't just look joyous, she was joyous! I guess that's why her beautiful smile was like a ray of sunshine on a cloudy day. It just made you feel good all over and warm inside. God can use anything to bring glory to Himself, and He used Monique's smile to brighten your day, to wipe away your tears, to make you smile, and to feel His love, peace, and presence. When you think of Monique, honor her with a SMILE!

Michelle Cervantes

Simply Unique

At certain times, I miss you the most. It is true you are in Heaven, but still, I brag and boast that I was lucky enough to know you. Your smile was the greatest thing to catch my eye. It's a shame we had to say goodbye. You were so elegant and full of grace. You always were able to put a smile on my face. So many wonderful things to say; so many memories have been made. I replay them over and over again. You were a truly great friend. Whenever I needed someone, you were there and always helped wipe away the tears. I can still feel your presence. I know that you're near. When I look at the clouds, I feel that you are looking down at me from my head to my feet, reminding me everything is going to be okay. I still see your awesome smile, which makes me feel better for a while. You were simple yet unique. Better yet, you were Monique.

Serena

The Remembering

You were just a freshman in Silhouettes,
So excited and young.
A new adventure to embark upon, To sing
and have some fun.
Every day you'd come into room 506,
Ready to sing your part,
Smiling that infectious smile,
That came straight from inside your heart.
I couldn't help but be your friend.

I don't think anyone could. Not after they
really knew you,
The you that was so good.
Every performance I knew you'd be there,
Doing the best you could do.
I would never worry, "Where's
Monique?" Your loyalty was always true.
Your smiles, hugs, and positive vibes, Will
be remembered through many years. Just
know that our love and memories Will last
longer than our tears.
Amanda

Million Dollar Smile

What can I say about Monique that already hasn't been said? Monique was gorgeous, wonderful, and a really nice person. If you ever heard her sing, she would have taken your breath away. Not only did she sing like an angel, she also looked like one. She was so hilarious and would make your stomach hurt from all the laughing. I miss her with all my heart. She is always a part of my thoughts.

Monique was my idol. She inspired me to be who I was, not who I was not. When you were down, she would smile at you, and her smile would force you to smile back. I always said that she had a million-dollar smile. When you saw her smile, you could not help being happy. Monique always was good and helpful to others. She would create dances and show them to my mom and me. She could dance so well, she taught my mom and me. Most of all,

Monique could brighten even the darkest room with her million-dollar smile.

Unknown

Last Words

I know that all of us have stories of the last conversation we had with Monique. I was one of the few blessed enough to speak to her after she went home from the hospital, but before she went home to meet her Father! I live in Texas and was not able to see her while she was in the hospital, but I spoke to her by phone a few times, and spent hours on the phone with her mom, keeping each other encouraged, together in prayer. Her mom and I have always been so close that I could picture everything she told me. It almost seemed as though I had actually been a part of everything Monique experienced in her life because of how vividly I was able to imagine what her mom shared with me.

But none of that could compare to the vividness I experienced when I spoke to Monique the day before she went to her Father for eternity. As I spoke to her, I told her about her cousins who were singing at a school performance that day, wanting to share because I knew how much she loved to sing. I told her I would video tape it, so the she could watch it the next time we saw each other, and in my mind, I could see her beautiful, smiling face.

But in my heart, I believed her spirit knew she was going to experience God soon because she didn't respond in the usual, "Yeah, I can't wait to see it," that I expected . . . she giggled instead, and I not only saw that beautiful smile, but I could picture her glowing! People always talk about how you can see the love of the Lord on someone because they have an almost angelic glow. On that day, I saw it in my mind, and felt it in my heart and soul. I knew that Monique was a child of the living God. I knew that her love for Him could not be quenched by any fiery darts that Satan would attempt to throw her way.

I told her how happy I was to hear her voice and laughter, and how proud I was of her for moving her mountain. We ended our conversation soon afterwards. I thank God everyday that I had the opportunity to tell her how much I loved her. Every time I think of her or see her pictures, I can hear her last words to me, "I love you, too, Tia!"

Stephanie

Chapter Eight

When Words are not Enough

"But the word of God continued to increase and spread."

—Acts 12:24 NIV

What more can a person say when all is said and done? As hard as we may try, there are no words that can fully express our pain, our sorrow, or our loss. Monique is with the Heavenly Father. But as we remember her words and the things, she tried to teach us, we must do more than simply remember. Words are not enough! The best way to honor Monique and her memory is to try our best to live our lives the way she lived hers. If Monique did something that turned your life around, why not pass that blessing onto another? Those of you who have lost a child, why not dedicate a change in your life to that child? For you know, all children are God's little angels. We must not be afraid to show our love for Our Savior. "For whoever is ashamed of Me and My words, the Son of Man will be ashamed of him when He comes in His glory, and the glory of the Father and of the holy angels." (Luke 9:26) We should be like Monique in professing our love for Jesus by both actions and words. Does this mean you have to drop everything and go about preaching like the Disciples? Not necessarily. Monique didn't. But if we can be a living example of Our Lord's love to all we come in contact with, just think how much we could change the world.

If Monique, who was still a child, could touch so many lives in so brief a time, and have such a powerful effect, how many more lives could those of us who will live seventy, eighty years, or more change? Can we change everyone? Unfortunately, not, but if each of us manages to change even one person and bring him or her closer to God, the end result would still prove powerful. Sometimes, all it takes is a little positive action.

No Known Definition

Just saying her name gives me a special feeling. The thought of her being gone is so hard but I'll try to express myself. There are no exact words to define Monique. When I met her, she was just a little girl, only seven years old, yet so smart and talented. She was full of spirit and always had a smile on her face, just full of life. My girls got along well with her because she was so friendly.

As time went by, we became very close, and it seemed to me that she was part of my family. We spent a lot of time together as a family, her sister Bianca, Brother Jacob, and my girls. Monique always stood out from everyone else, just like an angel. As time passed, we went through some personal problems, and Monique had an answer to everything. To her, there was always a way out.

She had a saying, "Everything will be all right," no matter what the situation.

She was always singing and dancing. Since she knew I was sentimental, everything she sang made me cry, simply because I knew she was growing up minute-by-minute. She meant so much to me that I didn't want to see her grow up. And yet, she was becoming a young lady. She continued to be the greatest example to everyone. She was one of a kind, she was smart and talented. There are no other words to describe Monique.

Unknown

Indescribable

My ideal purpose, as I write this piece, is to steer clear of cliché. I can present the grand compliments about Monique and use the words, "nice," "sweet," "funny," and all that mediocre mumbo jumbo that is said about everyone who has been uplifted from this life that we live. But I will do my best not to because in no way was Monique a cliché.

Everyone is nice, sweet, and just so wonderful. But Monique was way above that. She crossed the barrier of being a nice, sweet girl. She was nice to people because if she wasn't, she would feel like a terrible person. She was a friend to people in all shapes and sizes because she felt it was her duty in life. She was a beautiful person because that was who she was. It was in her character to have an open heart and to be a light to the world.

I wish there were words to make her standout above everyone, but I don't think there are. Maybe that's why she was so special. I honestly don't believe the love that shone through her so vibrantly was her intent. She never meant to give it. She was such an angel in this world that not much effort came out of her heart. Don't misconstrue my words and argue that I am professing that she didn't go out of her way for people. I am saying that she did so much for people, but once again, out of her character, not duty.

Life is simple and so is writing this. If you and I are in the flesh, then trying to express my feelings about Monique would be baffling. I would be trying to find the precise words. I would have you with me all day just so I can tell you: *Monique was indescribable.*

Jesse

A Walk Remembered

Monique Ashley Perez lived her life to the fullest. Even though she passed away young, she did what God wanted her to do on earth. I loved Monique. She absolutely changed my life!

Monique had a passion and drive in her for God like no other. Loving God and worshipping Him was one of her top priorities. Whenever I saw her, she talked about saving one of her friends or meeting new people. I have so many memories of Monique in the years that I knew her. Not only are they good memories, but they are filled with joy and laughter!

I remember when she would write and draw all over her pants. It was so much fun doing that with her. Even the smallest thing she did made an impact on me. I remember Sunday mornings, I would go to her house with my mom, dad, and sister after church at World Harvest Christian Center and we would just lounge around, have a cook-out, go down to their apartment's pool and have the best memories with her. Sometimes, we would come over on a week day and watch Monique wake up from her afternoon nap; she would come into the living room with a tank top, a pair of sweats, and her hair in pigtails. She would walk into the kitchen, grab a piece of white bread, and eat like never before.

Another good memory I have of her is when she showed us her eighth-grade graduation dress. She walked out of her bedroom and into the kitchen, wearing her black and white polka dot, frilly dress with her world-famous Converse shoes that had a whole bunch of writing and drawings on them, and she said, "Do you like it?" I couldn't say anything back. I had no words. That was Monique.

One thing I know about her was she didn't care what others thought about her, not one bit. I don't think she cared if her hair was a mess, or what shoes she was wearing, or even if she matched. As long as she was saving and impacting lives, that's all that mattered.

The last time I saw Monique was in the middle of the night. I was moving to Connecticut because of a family tragedy, and she handed me a blanket to stay warm within the car. I still have it to this day, and I always will. It's very hard to come to the reality about Monique's passing because she was so young. We all have our numbered days and these were hers.

When I'm feeling sad or down about her, I listen to her favorite songs and suddenly, I get a sense of peace that she will always be with me in my heart, along with all the memories we had together. It was very hard for me when I found out she had passed, A song that helped me through my grieving time and does so even now, is a song by Amy Grant called *Somewhere Down the Road.* I know she'll be there. She's like the wind. I can't see her, but I can feel her. I think about her always and the love that I had for her will never change! I loved her with all my heart.

She gave me the courage, grace, passion, and fire for God that I have today! She helped me get there! I've always wanted to be just like her; she's one of my heroes and she always will be! I realized that I could never be like her. She was herself, and no one can ever replace her. All I can do is keep her alive here on earth, and talk about her as much as possible. Not only will I love and miss her forever, I realized that Monique Perez's life was really a walk to remember! I love you Monique! I'll always remember you!

Briana

La Luna

There are some little things about Monique that matter so much to me. When I look-up into space, I feel a sense of joy and happiness. I feel love, and nothing else matters for the moment. I remember during high school, every day before Monique change into her P.E. clothes, we would look up to see if the moon was visible during the day. If we could see the moon, we would get excited and say, "There it is!" Those moments spent smiling and giggling with each other are some of my favorite memories. I am a Marine, and whenever I find myself patrolling at night or stationary, I glance up at the moon and the stars, and I go back to that moment in time.

Tony

Forever Missed

I still remember the day I learned she was gone. I couldn't believe an angel with a voice like hers was no longer with us. I would talk to her in class about this one guy she liked. I remember the service we had at school for her; everyone was crying, and I felt like she was there with us. I recall being there and crying because I knew I wouldn't have a friend like her around anymore. She was the kind of girl who had something great to say about everyone. She helped out with anything and everything. I really miss hearing her beautiful voice. She was truly an angel.

God Bless You and Forever Missed,

Antoinette

The eyes are the gateway to the soul

Monique with her Brother Jacob, to say they were close
is an understatement

Monique with little sister Bianca's 9th birthday. She always had a way of making things special for her.

A conqueror, a revolutionary and a teenager with a heart for God

Monique and Andy, 2003 Senior Prom

From left to right Bianca, Lydia, Bill, Jacob and Nathan at the 2006 Walk of Champion, in remembrance of those who lost the battle and those who continued the fight. For our family and others who came to celebrate the lives of their children.

Monique as a member of the Silhouettes Vocal group

Chapter Nine

The Real Deal

"Then Peter came to Jesus and asked, "Lord, how many times shall I forgive my brother when he sins against me? Up to seven times?" Jesus answered, "I tell you, not seven times, but seventy-seven times."

—Matthew 18:21-22 NIV

"God so loved the world that He sent His only Son so that sins may be forgiven." It is utterly mind-blowing when you consider the sacrifice our Lord made for us. Think about those He forgave: thieves, prostitutes, sinners of all kinds. "How blessed is he whose transgression is forgiven, whose sin is covered!" (Psalm 32:1). As ordinary humans, we often find it much harder to forgive those who sin against us. No one said it would be easy.

Monique, a child, was able to do just that. She forgave many people who hurt her, people who were supposed to be Christians, those who should have known better. Monique followed in Jesus' footsteps. She felt that if Our Savior could forgive those who tortured and murdered Him, how could she not forgive those who had wronged her? Those are high ideals for one so young. It's tough to forgive, even tougher to forget, but God asks us to do just that, and really, it all comes back to love. If we love one another, we should be able to forgive.

Of course, a perfect love would mean being extra careful not to hurt another person. But as frail human beings, that is a difficult task. Sometimes we hurt others simply because we didn't think before we spoke or acted. Maybe if we can perfect our love for God and each other, we can avoid hurting others. And whenever someone does slip, our love should give us the courage to forgive and forget. We must remember that when we hurt someone, we hurt God as well. So when we find ourselves needing to forgive another, just remember the Lord's Prayer: " . . . And forgive us our trespasses as we forgive those who trespass against us." We are often the ones who need to be forgiven. Holding hate and anger in your heart will drive love away. Hate and anger hurt not only those we direct it toward, but they also hurt us. These things poison us and make us miserable. Isn't love much better?

The Real Deal

I don't even know how to begin to describe Monique, because anything I say could not come close to doing her justice. She was an amazing young lady. The one thing I can say is that she was the same person to everyone she met. She didn't put on an act, depending on who she was with at the moment. I was just taken aback when I saw how much her friends loved her (at the memorial service at school, the viewing, and the funeral). Even though I wasn't part of her everyday life like her friends, I could see they saw the same qualities in her that I did.

She was genuine; what you saw was what you got. She truly lived God's greatest commandment . . . to love your neighbor as yourself. I'm sure that everyone will talk about her beautiful smile and the way it made their day brighter. Knowing this shows me that she was "the salt of the earth and the light unto the world." She displayed God's love in a way that many of us can only hope to emulate. She had such an awesome revelation of who and what God is, and His will for her life. She knew that she could do all things through Christ, who strengthened her. Because of this, she was able to face the knowledge of having leukemia without having fear.

Of course, she was human. One time while she was in the hospital, she was feeling down and tired, she didn't feel like doing anything. In fact, she didn't even want to take a shower, which was totally not her! I had the opportunity to talk to her and remind her that ever since she was young, she was never one to take anything lying down and that "can't" was not a part of her vocabulary, and not an option. The next thing I heard, she was out cruising the oncology floor!

Stephanie

Christ-Like

My name is Carlos Bojorquez, and I've known Monique since eighth grade. She was a great friend of mine. She didn't know I had a big crush on her in eighth grade. She was always there for me. Monique always had something positive to say even if she was the one with the bad day. She was very uplifting to me, and I really miss her. Monique always talked about Jesus to her friends.

To be real, just her lifestyle made me want to be more of a Christian. Her way of life was an example of how to become Christ-like. Truly, she was Christ-like. She always had something positive to say and was happy, no matter what she going through. She gave me advice even when she was the one feeling down. I truly miss her.

Carlos

Optimism

I first met Monique the day I went into Ladies in Harmony to tell her, along with a few other girls, that she had been accepted into Silhouettes. She was extremely excited to come into the group; she worked hard as one of the stronger singers in her section. Monique could be counted on everyday to have a smile on her face, no matter what was going on. Even if she was having a stressful day, she had a hug to give everyone, and a funny story to brighten up your day.

As a person, Monique strived to do her best in everything. The last time I saw her she told me all about her plans to finish the school year in independent study and come back the next year. Even in the face of trial, Monique's optimism could not be crushed. Her quiet spirit and strong faith are remembered fondly by many.

Amanda

Triad

Monique's life will always be remembered by us in three words: joyful, helpful, and mature. We never saw her down. She was always smiling, and her joy was contagious. Monique had a willing heart to help others and to fill in and volunteer where help was lacking. There were many times at church when we asked her to help; she never hesitated. She always said "Yes." The maturity Monique possessed reflected someone who was older than a teenager. She conducted her life as a great example not only to her peers but to those of us who are "older." Monique leaves us with an impression of God's grace to be imitated.

Ramon and Kellie

Supernatural

If you were to take a poll across the United States, asking parents if their kids are special, I believe every parent would say, "Yes, of course, my kids are special." Every child is special because he or she is a creation of God. We are given the opportunity and blessing to have them for only a little while. They are "on loan," if you will.

This is the life and testimony of Monique Ashley Perez. She came into this world extraordinary, and she left this world extraordinary. Monique entered this world, destined to be a people changer. She was a revolutionary. This sweet, beautiful creation of God had a way of changing the lives of those whose paths crossed with hers.

At first glance, people might have found her to be interestingly odd. But as you got to know her, you began to notice that she was always happy. You have never seen a smile so electrifying.

It is rare to find a person so young with a heart so committed to her relationship with God. She transformed her friends in a subtle way. Monique would say to them, "Remember to kiss your mom's goodbye." Her friends, at first, thought what a dork! Before you knew it, though, they were all kissing their mom's goodbye. Monique was the ultimate ambassador from God. She shared the Lord's love with people in a relevant, natural way. Life was not about going to church on Wednesdays and Sundays. Monique's life was about her love for God seven days a week, twenty-four hours a day. Those who knew her as well as those who had just met her found something irresistible about her. Yes, she was irresistible in a Godly way. She was real. She was supernatural.

Bill Maeda

Forgiveness

"When you are praying, First forgive anyone
that you are Holding a grudge against so that
your father in Heaven Will forgive your
sins, too."

Mark 11:25 NLT

Monique was, without a doubt, a true imitator of God. We believe that she found it easy to forgive people who had greatly wronged her, as she would imitate the attributes of Jesus Christ. In a very short time, we witnessed this daughter of God abused in so many different ways, in places where you would think that abuse should not be seen. Within the youth group that she was so committed to, there were promises easily made and more easily broken. She was ignored by those who called her their friend, and excluded from going out with the girls, just because.

We have never seen a girl cry so often or get her feelings hurt so frequently. We witnessed a youth leader say that she had many years of experience with teenagers and that only bad fruit would come from Monique's life. Her trust was violated by sharing with another and then finding that the words so easily spoken in confidence were splattered all about the church, deeply entrenched in the rumor mill. This is not a condemnation of anybody or any organization. For we know there is no condemnation. This is a reflection of a daughter of Christ, who no matter what or how she was abused, rose to the top and sprouted forth the most excellent fruit. In the midst of the abuse, broken promises, and breach of trust, Monique never failed to forgive. We recalled a phone conversation where Monique was overheard saying, "Don't cry. It's okay. I forgive you."

We wonder as adult Christians what it takes to develop this degree of forgiveness. We asked Monique once how she found it so easy to extend forgiveness to those who had hurt her. We got into a conversation about the movie "The Passion." The end result of our conversation went like this: With all that was done to Jesus before and during the crucifixion, he was still willing to extend forgiveness for all who would ask. Monique said to us, "Nothing anybody could do to me could be any worse than what was done to Jesus." "So, if Jesus could forgive, then I should be willing to forgive also." Monique said, "You silly goose," and literally skipped away. We think about it today; Monique was fifteen years old, but she had a well-developed spiritual maturity. She continues to inspire.

Lydia and Bill Maeda

Nothing Missing   Nothing Broken

One of the awesome benefits of having a relationship with God is living a healthy physical life. It is God's intention that you are healthy and whole with nothing missing and nothing broken, and that you are well from the top of your head to the very soles of your feet. People often pray, *"God's will be done."* His will is for you to be healthy and whole, and that we not know sickness in our lives. It is God's will and his desire for us that we live a life of faith in divine health.

Monique had an uncompromising faith in healing. As parents who equally share this faith of healing, it sometimes is hard for us to understand how we lost our daughter to a disease. Monique did not pick or choose from the Bible. What is said in the Bible is what she believed. Doubt did not exist in her life. It wasn't part of her vocabulary, nor did it ever exit her mouth. Monique was not selfish about her faith in healing. She wanted everyone to know that healing in Jesus could be just as real to them as it was to her.

We had gone to see a guest speaker at a local church. Monique was only eleven at the time. The service concluded, and the Pastor gave a huge altar call for anyone believing in healing. Monique's brother Jacob had asthma, and she tried to get him to go to the healing line, but he wouldn't. We had a nebulizer at home to assist Jacob's breathing. Like most kids, the last thing he wanted to do was to put an oxygen mask on his face. Monique always kept a close eye on Jacob while he played. She would sit with him during his treatments and put the oxygen mask on, pretending she was getting a breathing treatment. Then she would tell him that he was next.

Monique looked at Jacob and said, "Okay, I'll pray for you right here." She placed her hands on his shoulders and began praying. I could hear her saying in a soft, sweet voice, "Receive your healing now." It has been eight years since Jacob used his nebulizer. When I noticed that Jacob did not need the machine any longer, I mentioned it to Monique, but she gave me this look that said, "Of course, he does not need it anymore. He prayed, and God healed him." The will of God was done in Jesus' name. Restoration received, nothing missing nothing broken.

Mom . . .

Chapter Ten

A Family Affair

**"... *sorrowful, yet always rejoicing; poor,*
yet making many rich; having nothing, and
yet possessing everything."**

—Corinthians 6:10 NIV

Death always brings sorrow, yet we are told to rejoice. "... but to the degree that you share the sufferings of Christ, keep on rejoicing, so that also at the revelation of His glory you may rejoice with exultation (Peter 4:13). Thanks to the sacrifice Our Lord made for us, we can rejoice, even though we are sorrowful when we lose someone we love. Sometimes, our sorrow is more for ourselves because we must now wait to see our loved one again, but we must take comfort in the fact that our dearest has gone to Heaven and is now happy and safe with the Lord. No more sorrow, pain, unhappiness, fear, or uncertainty will ever touch them again.

Remembering the happy, funny, and unique times we spent with someone who has passed is one of the ways we have to help us through the loss. A funny story or a shared joke often eases the pain, if only briefly. Later, those memories help keep that person alive in our hearts and minds, and we find that we can smile as we share a memory or gaze lovingly at a picture and remember the tiny slice of life that accompanied it.

As much as we want to be with that loved one again, we must not let the desire become so overwhelming that we forget that God still has a purpose for us—a reason to keep us here a little longer. He does not want to pine away or destroy our lives because He has called our dear one home before us. Jesus wants us to honor their memory by living a life dedicated to Him, so when He decides to call us home, we can join Him and our dearly departed, and live together for eternity in His joy, peace, and love.

Most Fun with Monique

One of the things Monique and I did together that I would consider one of the best times ever was when we joined a gym. We signed up for a Latin Aerobics class. For those of you who know Monique, you know she did not need to lose weight, but she did it to encourage me. We had such a blast!! The classes were Tuesdays and Thursday at 7:00 p.m. I worked-out; trying to keep-up with the class, but Monique was actually dancing like she was at a party. She would say, "Come on, mom."

During the warm-up part and running, Monique would stay behind with me. She never really liked running. When we needed to be in pairs, we would always make sure we were together. One time, we were using the Chinese rope in which we had to put it around our waists and pull backwards. She was so light. I pulled her clear to my side. We laughed so hard, we left the class. We would just look at each other and start laughing, unable to concentrate.

When class was over, we would sit on the bicycles and people watch. We would make comments like, "Wow, that looks hard. Or maybe we should try that next". She would look at me and say, "NAW!" And we would both laugh. One time, we did not take the dance class, but sat on the bicycles and talked about school, work, church, and life. We were having such a good and serious conversation. Monique looked at me and said, "Mom, we have been sitting for almost a half hour and are barely pedaling the bikes. I thought there were people waiting to use the bikes. Is this doing anything for us?" I looked at her and said, "Physically, not a darn thing."

We started laughing, then we tried to race on the bikes, but all we could do was laugh. Monique had trouble keeping her feet on the pedals. She was going so fast, I was struggling, going much slower. We decided it was time to get off the bikes. Monique said, "Mom, let's walk around the gym like we have been working out hard. So, we did. Every time someone asked if we need anything Monique would answer, "We just finished using that machine, but thanks."

The best part of those nights was when we left the gym. On the way home, Monique would ask in a small voice, "Mom, can you take me to McDonalds?" Then she would ask, "You aren't going to eat anything?" And I would reply, "I can't, they are waiting for me at home." Then we would walk back to the car, and she would give me a huge hug, and say, "Thanks, Mom." Then she would add, "McDonalds will be our little secret."

Lydia . . . A grateful mom

My Granddaughter

My daughter Lily was pregnant with our very first grandchild. I wanted to be the first one to hear my granddaughter Monique cry. I kept walking up and down the hallway, hoping to be able to hear her. At the time, my son Ninos had to go to court to pay a traffic ticket. It was close to the hospital, so my husband took him to court. Once they returned, I was walking back to the room to check on Lily, and there was Ninos, standing there saying, "Mom, the baby was born." My son was the first to hear Monique cry. I guess being second was ok.

Grandma Mary

Gray Hairs

When Monique came to this world, you could tell she was so special. After she was born, she stayed at our house for a few months. We enjoyed that little baby so much. I remember many beautiful, wonderful things about my granddaughter.

When Monique was older, I use to talk to her on the phone. I would ask her what she was doing. Her answer was almost always the same. She would say, "I'm doing my homework." She was always going somewhere or doing something for the school or the church.

I use to tell her she was too good, and that she should do something to give her mother a few gray hairs. My little baby would say, "Grandpa, I can't do that!" "Of course", I would say, "It's easy. Let me show you how." Once, I told her to go outside and flirt with the little boys, so that her mom would get angry. I told her, "See all my gray hairs? They're from your mom and your uncles." Monique would always reply, "Grandpa, I can't do that!" She knew I was just kidding her. I loved to joke around with Monique just to hear her laugh. The only way we can handle the loss of our little baby is by knowing she is in Heaven making Jesus laugh. You made us very happy, and always found a way to make everybody happy. I will always remember Monique saying, "Grandpa! Don't be mean to Grandma." I am so happy and proud of Monique.

One of these days, we will be together, and I will remind her to give her momma a few gray hairs.

Grandpa "Tony"

Pillow talk

It took me a while to even be able to talk about my sister. I didn't even want to be reminded of her, because it was so hard. Now I find myself thinking of her from time to time, and I can smile and sometimes laugh. The one memory I have that makes me laugh is when we lived in the old apartment. One night, Monique and I were having a pillow fight and were running through the apartment being silly, hitting each other with pillows. I saw Monique run and hide on the side of the wall in the hallway. Suddenly, Mom turned the corner, and Monique swung the pillow as hard as she could, hitting Mom in the face. Mom fell back and hit the wall. Monique eyes opened wide.

She was shocked to learn she had hit Mom. I just stood in the hallway watching, and thought my mom was going to cry. Mom was so mad; she took the pillow and hit Monique. Monique went flying; she fell so hard that I thought Mom had hurt her. Monique laid on the bed with her head down like she was crying. She looked through her fingers to see where our mother was. Once she knew she had left, she lifted her head and burst-out laughing. It was so hilarious.

Sometimes you might think of Monique was fragile or weak, but NO WAY! She was strong when she wanted and very funny. I will never forget the look on Monique's face when that pillow hit Mom's face.

Best memories and good times.
Always in my heart,
Your brother, Jacob

Fun Times

Monique was more than just my daughter. She also was a friend who encouraged me. I raised and taught her as a child, and she had rules. As she began to grow, I realized she was more than my child; she was my best friend. As she grew, we mostly talked about life, and spent a large amount of time together. We watched television together and really liked sentimental movies. I recall sitting in the movie theater. We would look at each other, knowing what the other was thinking, and she would give me a big smile and say, "Mom, you're going to cry, huh?" My eyes would get watery, and we would both start laughing.

One thing I really respected about Monique was that every time she went to a special dance or event, she would always ask me to take her to the store and help her choose an outfit. She seemed to value my opinion, which I thought was great. Most teenage girls do not seem to like there moms' opinion. As a parent, you would think that it was our job to make our kids feel special. Yet, Monique had a way of making me feel special, just by including me in her life.

Even as a child in elementary school, I had to stop going to her field trips because every time I went, she would just stay by my side. I would tell her it was okay to sit with her friends, or go play, but she always wanted to stay with me. I felt as though I was keeping her from time with her peers, but she continued this way through her teen years.

I went with her on a field trip when she was in Junior High. I was the only parent besides the teachers. I felt so good that she included me. We had a great time. Sometimes when I think of her, I remember one of our favorite movies, "When Fools Rush In." There is a part in the movie where the wife is in the kitchen cooking. She does not realize her husband is home, and she is dancing around to Salsa music. As a result, every now and then when I would be cooking and Monique was helping me or washing the dishes, I would look at her, and we would begin dancing our salsa moves. We would start laughing, and say "I knew you were going to do that." It was awesome to be so connected with each other that we didn't even have to say anything. We knew exactly what the other was going to do.

Mom

Sister Stuff

To me, there are a lot of special things about my sister, probably too many to write. Every time I think of her, something new comes to mind. One thing that was special was when Mom would work on Saturdays. I would wake-up, run into Monique's room, and get under the blankets with her. We would watch TV, staying in bed till almost 1:00 p.m., and then she would ask if I was hungry. She would get up and make us a sandwich. It was so warm and cozy. We both loved watching cartoons and movie after movie. It was the best sister-to-sister time ever.

One thing between my sister and I that I miss is when she would act like she was picking her nose and then she would chase me around and wipe her finger on me. To this day, I do not know if she was really picking her nose or pretending. She usually did it when I was sad or mad and it was her way to get me to laugh and forget what had upset me.

I miss my sister very much. I don't think a day goes go by that I do not think about her, especially when the day is not going well. There was a time I was very sad, missing her a lot, and she came to me in a dream. It was so real; I will never forget. We were both younger, and in the dream, she came to me and said, "Hi, baby girl. Can I lay with you?" Then she crawled into my bed on our sides with our legs bent, and she would hug me, just the way we always did. She made me laugh, and I could hear her laughing.

Just then she told me that whenever I wanted to remember the good times, all I had to do was to go to the time machine, and it would show me and take me to the fun times we had together and I would feel her near. Then she asked if I was hungry. I said, "Yes," and she said she would be back. She was going to make me a sandwich. She walked away and I woke up. I was so happy and grateful that she had come to me. It let me know everything will be okay and that she was always going to be near.

Monique had a way of making any day special. It never cost her much, just her time and heart. On my ninth Birthday, she made me a huge poster with pictures of friends and family, and then took it down to the pool where we were having the party. She had all my guests sign it. When they sang "Happy Birthday," she smashed my face into the cake. Every year on my birthday, I take out the poster and put it on the table with my cake. For me, it is like having her there. Of all the things she ever bought or gave to me, this poster means the most. Like my sister would always say, "***I will keep this forever***

Love (baby girl) Bianca

Connection

Some people say that twins know what the other is thinking—that they even know how the other is feeling. Monique was my sister, and although we were not twins, I feel as though we had a really cool connection. It's like we knew each other better then we knew ourselves. She made me realize the importance of life and to appreciate what God has given us. Monique was the one person who influenced my life more than anyone. She showed me how to love and care for people. Whenever I was having a hard time, she gave me a reason to keep on going. She made me realize how important God can be in our lives, and how much he loves and can change us.

We had some really funny times. One day, we were walking home from elementary school and decided to hold hands, pretending we were boyfriend and girlfriend. She said, "Let's see what people will do, and if they say something to us because we are so young." You wouldn't believe all the cars that honked at us. We laughed and laughed. She had the best smile. Every time you saw her, she was smiling. The best times, though, where the times we would sit in her room, shut the door, and have brother/ sister talks. She understood me and always had a way of making everything better.

The one thing I will never forget about my sister was that regardless of who or what you are, she loved you, no matter what. Sometimes I like to keep my thoughts about my sister to myself, because they are important to me, and I get protective of my relationship with her. But the most important thing is that no one can ever compare or take the place of my sister, she is #1 to me.

Jacob

Big Sister

When the kids were small, I use to go to my mom's house every weekend. My parents lived about two-and-a-half hours from San Diego. Monique was always protective and very caring toward her brother. I remember when she was only two-and-a-half. We were on the way back from my parent's house, and Jacob started crying. He kept crying and crying. Monique was sitting in the back seat with him. He was only six months old, so he was sitting in the car seat. I could hear her talking to him and kept thinking to myself how much I really wanted to get home. Suddenly, he stopped crying. I thought, "Oh thank goodness, he finally fell asleep." When I got home, I opened the back door of the car to get Monique and Jacob, and there he was, sitting in his car seat, sucking on Monique's finger. She looked at me with those gorgeous eyes and said, "I couldn't find his pacifier." Then she smiled and said he's not crying anymore. So, for at least twenty to thirty minutes, she sat there letting him suck her finger. It was quite a sight. I just started laughing and said, "Thank you, baby, for helping with your brother."

Mom

Our Favorite Times

One of our most favorite things to do was going for walks. Monique would wait until right before dinner and say, "Grandma, let's go for a walk." Monique always wanted to go to McDonalds. She would order a hamburger, french fries, and of course, a coke. Sometimes we would just walk and walk. We would finally get around to walking home, then as soon as we arrived Lily would say, "Okay it's time for dinner." Monique would always say something like, "Oh, I'm not hungry." Later, I would tell Lydia that we went to McDonalds. These were my most favorite times of all.

Grandma

Special Moments

It would be impossible to count all the special moments that Monique and I were able to share together. One of my favorites was watching movies or love stories on the Lifetime Channel. I miss these special times, lying on the couch, sharing a blanket, and watching a good movie. We would cry and laugh together, and talk about what we would do if we were the ones in the movie. We would be on opposite sides of the couch, so it was hard to see each other's faces, but at just the right moment in the movie, we would turn to look at each other with watery eyes and start laughing. We knew what the other was thinking and feeling.

One of my favorite moments was tucking her in at night. I waited to hear her yell from her room, "Mom, Come and tuck me in." Sometimes if it was getting late, I would go to her room thinking she was already asleep, but she would be working on a project or watching a movie. When I told her that I thought she was already asleep, she would say, "How can I fall asleep if you haven't tucked me in?" I do not know if tucking her in was more for her or for me.

Mom

Chapter Eleven

Monique's Legacy

*"I have set you an example that you should
do as I have done for you."*

—John 13:15 NIV

As parents, the best way to teach our children the correct and proper way to conduct themselves in life is through example. Words are important, but they can ring hollow if what we say and what we do ends up being different. Jesus taught us to live by His example, and when we do, we also teach others His ways, especially our children. Monique seemed to know this instinctively. Yes, she told her friends, family, and siblings how to abide in Jesus. Monique talked the talk and she walked the walk. She modeled the message of living a life in Christ.

How many times have you told your children to stop fighting, but later began to fight with your spouse over something silly? It's no wonder the children become confused. You have just sent a mixed message. "Don't fight with each other, but it is okay if your dad and I fight." No, it isn't always easy to follow your own advice. But it should make us think about what we do before we do it, and how we might better achieve our purposes. Then again, maybe Monique had an advantage over most adults, simply because she was so young and insightful.

Monique accepted Jesus into her life. Quite simply, that acceptance, in her mind, meant that she had to live in a Christ-like manner. She never questioned it; she simply lived it. It is amazing the number of lives she touched and changed. It is even more amazing that those people continue to strive to be as Monique wanted them to be . . . Christ-like. Maybe she is an angel, but that is no excuse for the rest of us to slack-off. Jesus wants us to show our love for Him by following His example, and even if it takes the rest of our lives to perfect it that is exactly what we should do.

Monique Perez Award 2005

Before we present the Monique Perez award for the Outstanding Silhouette, my wife and I would like to take this opportunity to thank Kevin Willard for establishing the Monique Perez Scholarship fund, and of course, Mike Swift. You are gone but not forgotten. It was a year ago that we stood before you and presented this award for the first time. I think it was easier a year ago, since we still were in a state of numbness having just lost Monique and were searching for our own survival. Looking back, I see that we have just begun to realize the impact that one small girl had on the lives of so many people, including the students and staff of Chula Vista High School.

Monique often said that you were the most real people that she knew. She made a conscious decision to love people for who they were on the inside, rather than what they appeared to be on the outside. I would like you to know that at one point, I offered Monique the opportunity to go to any high school in the district. But she wouldn't hear of it. She couldn't conceive of being anything but a Spartan. Monique bled blue. She was a Spartan through and through.

I have come to realize that Monique got the most she could out of life. She lived life a little better every day as if it were the only day. She lived as though each day was created especially for her. Monique's life was about beauty, whether reflected in music, art, song, or the sheer beauty of life itself. So, I encourage you, not only as graduating seniors, but as underclassman and human beings to live each day like there is no tomorrow, because honestly, tomorrow may never come. Live responsibly but live your life without regret and never forget that you were loved, and are still loved, by one beautiful girl named Monique.

We would like to leave you with one thought before we present the award. Some of Monique's dearest friends created a memorial tee shirt about a year ago. This shirt said, "Monique is like the wind. You can't see it, but you can feel it." It is our great honor to present the 2005 Monique Perez Award for Outstanding Silhouette to Jessenia Robles.

Senior Class of 2006

Hello, class of 2006. Lydia and I are honored and privileged to share this time with you, our extended Spartan family. We would like to thank you for your support over the past years. The CVH's staff support has been unprecedented. We are honored to present the Monique Perez Award for the Outstanding Silhouette, which includes a $600 cash award.

This is a bittersweet time for us. We had expected our own daughter to be sitting among you. This was to be a time when we looked forward to the prom, graduation night, the whole senior year, watching our daughter graduate into adult life. Instead, we stand before you presenting this award in her honor—in her absence. Yet, this time is sweet because we are able to honor one among you who has set herself apart and was determined to be a Spartan of Excellence.

As the years passed, everything that needed to be said has been said, and everything that needed to be done has been done. So, we thought that as we stand before you tonight, we would encourage you as Monique would have encouraged you. As you leave behind the walls of Chula Vista High School and move forward into your adult lives, do not forget your dreams. Hold onto them . . . never surrender them to the pressures of adult life. We all must dream. We must keep a vision of something in our lives to reach for—something we strive for, something that pushes us and motivates us when our own motivation isn't quite enough. Hold onto your dreams and when you achieve them, dream bigger—for yourself and for your families.

Never stop, because when you stop dreaming, you cease to live.

As you move forward into your adult lives, there will be bumps in the road . . . be assured of this. Always know that Monique is watching over you, encouraging you to reach for more. The class of 2006 is unique. Some of you knew Monique back in elementary school. You are the last class that had a personal relationship and personal knowledge of her. This award will continue to be presented as the years pass. But it will be presented to a deserving person who did not know Monique. This makes you unique—a class of very special friends and teachers. So as this school year comes to a close, we take great pleasure in presenting the Monique Perez Award for Outstanding Silhouette to Angelique Pena.

Lydia and Bill Maeda

Newness of Life in Water Baptism

After attending World Harvest Christian Center for some time, Monique, Jacob, and I decided we would get water baptized. I had spoken with both of them and knew they understood what it meant to be baptized. When Monique's name was called, she went to the Pastor. He asked her, "What has God done for you since you accepted Jesus as your Lord and Savior?" Monique answered, "Jesus has taken away all my fears."

I just looked at her and felt proud, but at the same time wondered, "What fears?" I was doing everything that I possibly could to give my children a good, stable life.

Was I doing enough to make her feel safe and secure? I was determined not to let my children become a statistic of divorce. I always made sure whatever difficulty I was dealing with, not to let it show to my kids.

Then Monique said, "I know that no matter what, with God everything will be okay. He will always be there for me." At this point, I did not realize the wisdom and personal relationship she had with God. As I look back now, I see that even at the tender age of eleven, her complete trust was in Him. She was so mature in faith for her age. I saw her as my daughter that I was always proud of. I failed to see the awesome servant of God she was becoming. Even at eleven, she was aware of becoming a new creature in Christ. She understood that being water baptized was an act of obedience. It was an outward expression of what had happened to her spiritually. Romans 6:1-18 tells us about being buried with Him by baptism into death—that as Christ was raised up from the dead by the glory of the Father, we also should walk in the newness of life, and that is exactly what she did.

Mom

Tribute

Today was tragic. I don't even know where to begin. I suppose I should start from the beginning. It was 9:08 a.m., and I'm skipping second block because I'm sick. After I heard the news, I just got sick. A younger girl, who attended my school this year, passed away from leukemia. I was told the news instantly after arriving to second period, and it struck me hard. Ashley was crying badly, too. Knowing this, I had to run to the washroom, at least three or four times to throw-up or attempt to.

At least half the student body were in the halls in groups, crying. I cried as well. I guess I regret it. The occasional "hi" that we shared at football and basketball games wasn't enough, I suppose. I realize there should have been more than that. The potential and effervescence of this student were incredible. She was always full of life and never taking a moment for granted. She always tried to liven-up the situation and always had a smile on her face. I can see that many knew her.

I overheard a few girls in the hallway. One said that she used to hang out with her. Walking down the hall is so painful now, knowing that someone so young lost her life. And FOR WHAT? God knows it's just the way it is, I guess. I normally don't acknowledge a situation such as this, but I know what it's like to lose someone you love so much. If you see me in the hall or in the street, don't say a thing. I did this of my own free will, but if you need a hug, I'm here. If you need to talk, I'm here. We're all together when it comes to this. Even if you hate me or don't want to know me, just say "hi," because I can tell we are sharing the same pain.

This is a tribute to a girl I knew, a tribute to the life of someone who brought light into every life she encountered, even with her simple, beautiful, and unforgettable smile. This is a tribute from student to student. And this is a prayer to God. Take care of her. She truly blessed the hallways of Chula Vista High.

Remember all the good times you shared with her, because every life that she was in, she touched—even mine with her "hellos." Monique, I love you. And I know that one day we'll meet again. Tell my grandma I said "Hi."

I just wanted you to know that you'll never be forgotten. There never will be anyone as special as you. You truly were an angel God placed among so many lives. I still remember the argument we had in eighth grade English class about religion. Thanks for talking some sense back into me. I can't cry anymore; you are with the Lord and HAPPY. Tell the Big Man up there I said, "Thanks."

She deserves to be known.
Kourtney

Beautiful is She

Lord God of Heaven and Earth, Glorious Jesus, faithful friend and comforter, Savior, King of Kings, Lord of Lords, the only True and Living God, sweet and precious Heavenly Father, full of loving kindness, abundance of compassion, grace and tender mercies for all, no one goes without when they have you. How awesome you are in all you do for those who seek your face! Your heart and thoughts are for us. No one could truly understand.

Sweet Jesus, hear these words I pray in awe. We are the work of your hands. The masterpiece of your work leaves us with tears of joy and happiness. You orchestrate such glorious works that no one can stop speaking of them.

As we wait for your voice to lead us, we see your divine plan unfold, and cherish the work you give us to display. We give you thanks and continue to ask for your direction that the memory of our friend may live. The daughter and friend you gave us moved in us mightily! You set forth a plan and gave her direction to move in our lives, showing yourself through her, teaching, encouraging, counseling, crying, laughing, forgiving, loving, and giving grace and mercy to us.

She has done the work you asked of her and in awe of your presence, left this world behind and set forth to your kingdom with one thought in her mind and heart—Jesus! Lord, help us to bless your name, your kingdom, and all that you are as you have blessed us with the life of Monique Ashley Perez. You gave her a smile that illuminated the darkest room and the wisdom to know you. She lived a life of years beyond her age that touched so many and will live strong for you. For this we thank and praise you!

Her life and death brought changes to our lives, and those lives she touched will never be the same. She has changed us for the better in your glory that we would make a stronger stance for you, just as she did. We wanted what she had, and through her service to you, she showed us how to live, as she lived for you. May we live each day as she did, hugging and loving each other as we depart, remembering that our days are numbered and to always do the work of our Heavenly Father.

The life she lived was as normal as any teenagers with one big exception. She knew who she was because she had you, and it made her life stand-out. She was not ashamed but proud of the life you gave her, and she ran with the task at hand. She is beautiful. The lives she touched are precious because she introduced Jesus to us through her life, and when we depart this earth, she will be the one to introduce Jesus to us in our Heavenly home.

Lita

Never to Have Known her

There is a very well-known saying that states, "You do not know what you have until it is gone." From my point of view, I wouldn't say that I greatly underestimated the impact that Monique would have on the lives of the people she knew. What I underestimated was the impact that she has had on people who did not directly know her. It is truly amazing that she has worked in the lives of people on earth as well as in Heaven. I recall after Monique's going home service, my Mom came to me and said, "Billy, your brother Bob wanted you to know that he feels that he missed-out on something very special in life by not having the opportunity to know Monique."

This is amazing, since he never knew her. He was drawing from a memory shared with him by over 600 people who packed a small hall to express their love for her. I have heard this time after time. Monique was a world changer. She has just continued her work from Heaven. I think about her being a world changer, and maybe this is not the best description of Monique. She was a revolutionary spirit. She revolutionized your spirit in small ways by setting a Christ-like example. Monique transformed a person's spirit in a huge way, by sharing the love of God, being a Godly example, never compromising, and never ever giving up until Jesus became real to the people she loved, which, by the way, was everybody. I can safely say Monique is not only my hero, she is my example.

Bill Maeda / Grandma Tiny

Phenomenal

I was crying, scared, nervous, confused, shocked, mad, and frustrated. I was in denial. I was feeling every feeling I had ever felt before in a single night. The pain was unbearable—the desire to run and hide was knocking at my door. Luckily, the friend that broke the news to me was smart enough to ask for my car keys before he told my brother and me, because I would have driven as far away as I could. Watching my brother Andy as he lay on the floor crying and hyperventilating was adding to the pain, because I knew how badly he was hurting, and it made me hurt even more.

I tried to be strong and keep everyone else sane while I knew I wanted answers. I wanted peace, and I wanted Monique to be there. Instead, the paramedics showed-up at my door to give my brother breathing assistance. After they left, I continued to cry. The pain continued the next morning. I had received a call from Lydia. She wanted to tell us before we found out from someone else, but it was too late. We had already cried for about ten hours and continued to hurt. She asked my brother and me if we would help carry the casket. I wasn't sure if I could handle it, but I was willing to do anything for Monique.

My brother and I agreed. Not only did we agree, but we also wanted to do something else. So, we came up with the idea of putting on the memorial service at her school, which also was the high school that Andy and I graduated from. A few days after her death, my brother and I found ourselves sitting in the office with the principal of the high school. We asked if we could arrange a service at the high school during school hours. He told me to write a proposal and to bring it back to him the following week. The next morning, I was back in his office with the proposal in my hand. We told him we wanted to do it before the viewing. He was shocked. He had expected us to delay it for a couple weeks. But we were serious, so he agreed to let us do it that week. We were able to take the Praise and Worship Band that Monique used to lead into the high school. It was one of the hardest moments I had on stage, because the emotions were so strong. We led the students in a worship service with a short message by our youth pastor. We know that lives were changed, and that God got hold of some people, not because of the music and speaking, but because of the focus that was placed on Monique and the things that were said about her.

After wards we went to the viewing. It was an unbelievable sight. There were over seven hundred people. The lines went out the door. There were family and friends everywhere, and it made me realize that my life wasn't the only one that Monique had touched. She lived the difference and brought Heaven to earth. It made me so happy to know that her short life was not a life lived in vain. It made me excited, and it made me thank God that a person like Monique was able to walk this earth, speak to people's lives, and change them by just being the person that God created her to be.

To this day, there are people that still go to church because of the Christ-like example Monique lived by. At the funeral, you would have thought the President had died. There were so many people. It was hard to believe she was only fifteen years old. It has now been about four years since this happened. Every time I think about it, I still recall how amazing she was, and how lucky I was to be able to call her one of my great friends—a friend that was willing to listen to me and encourage me, a friend that was willing to tell me to shut-up when I was being stupid, and a friend that was not scared to give up her time for her friends. She was a true friend.

A lot has changed in my life since her passing. I got married, relocated, and I'm starting a family of my own. My wife and I have a daughter, and we named her Monique. Monique's story is worth telling everyone—one that I will continue to share with my kids and grandkids. I'm just thankful that I was able to be friends with her, and that she was able to meet my amazing wife. Monique would call me when she was in the hospital and tell me that her nurse reminded her of my wife. She also told the nurse that she reminded her of her friend's wife, who was in Australia. The nurse thought Monique was crazy, wondering how a fifteen-year-old could have friends in Australia. The nurse actually thought Monique was getting high off the medication and was just talking mindlessly while she was out of it.

On another occasion, I remember when my wife and I took Monique and my brother out to eat. On the way back to the car, Monique and my brother where walking behind us and Monique turned to my brother and said, "Dang, baby got back!" She was referring to my wife's behind. We could not stop laughing. Monique was so fun to be around, and fun to talk with. She kept the conversation moving forward. I really miss Monique, and I can't wait to see her again in Heaven. It's going to be so awesome. We will have so much to catch-up on, and so much to experience together. I really hope that by sharing my perspective of Monique, I was able to share with you how much Monique meant to me. All I can say now is . . . she's awesome, an incredible person . . . phenomenal.

Jose

A Dream

I had a dream one night shortly after Monique went home to God. I dreamed we were hanging out together, talking. I recall that she was telling me to follow God and not to ever, ever stop following him. A few days passed, and I felt as though I was doing something wrong. I felt a conviction about something that I had never felt bad about before. I confessed to my mom and shared my dream with her. My mom confirmed that what I was doing was wrong, and I made the choice to stop then and there.

I believe that God gave me this dream because He knew I would listen to Monique. Monique had a way about her that made you want to listen. She would get you thinking about your decisions. I always viewed Monique as a good Christian with high standards. The dream was important to me, as it came from a very important person in my life, not from a stranger, relative, or adult. The dream spoke of care and concern for me.

Israel

Best Friends

When I first met Monique and Lydia, I loved the relationship they had with each other. They were best friends, yet they also were mother and daughter. This type of relationship is not something you see very often. I did not have that kind of closeness with my mother, and I admired what they had and desired it. You could tell they were comfortable with each other and confident with whom they were. Monique could be herself with her mom. She was comfortable telling her mother anything, even receiving constructive criticism, or when talking to her mother about her true feelings.

Monique's mother took all that her daughter was as if that was herself. She truly valued her as if Monique was who she was. That truly is what our Lord Jesus tells us to do with each other: To value others more than ourselves and treat them the way you want to be treated. Yet these days, you do not see this very often, nor do you see such closeness between a mother and daughter. Monique was not ashamed to be with her mother. She wanted to be with her. Teenage girls do not want to be seen with their mothers and do not want to talk with them about their lives these days.

Often, mothers are ashamed of their daughters because the daughter does not live up to their mom's expectations. Sometimes a teenage girl does not want her mother involved in her life, preferring to be left alone to do what she wants. Monique and Lydia's relationship was definitely one I wanted with my mother, and one I know every daughter and mother wants. It is the design God intends a mother and daughter to have, and Monique and Lydia had it! As a mother of two boys, I desire this closeness with my sons. Maybe someday when it is God's will, I will have a daughter like Monique, and I will be able to have the same relationship with my daughter as Monique had with her mom.

When Monique went home to be with the Lord, I was pregnant with my second son. I did not know at the time it was a boy. I really wanted a girl! I asked Lydia, "If I have a girl, could I name the baby after Monique?" I like to name my children after people who have a story to tell about their life, so that when my child asks me why I gave this name, I can say what it means to me and to other people. I can tell the story of their name. When God does give me a daughter, I hope to name her after Monique. She will grow up to be just like Lydia's Monique who touched so many lives the way God asked her to!

I cannot wait till that day God gives me a daughter, so I can tell her about the beautiful young lady she was named after, and why I chose her name.

In my eyes, Monique was an average teenager. Yet she had something that others needed and wanted, but do not realize. She was confident, smart, and had high self-esteem. She had a true relationship with Jesus, and she was proud of it. She was what I wanted to be when I was her age. I am thirty-two now, and I still want to be just like her. When Monique passed away, I cried as if she were my best friend and sister. I did not know her very well, but I knew God wanted me to.

Today, as I sit and write, I still cry because of whom she is today, and how she impacted my life. I wish I could have spent more time with her. Monique was beautiful inside and out, but more inside because she had Jesus within her. She was beautiful on the outside, yet her trust in the Lord added to her beauty. As humans, we first look at the outside with our eyes. Yet, Monique did as Jesus does; she looked at the inside with the eyes of his heart. She learned this from Jesus, and she taught it to others in her life. I am learning more and more about Monique as I hear the stories about her.

When she went home to be with the Lord, I cried and told Jesus I wanted to be just like her. Jesus told me, "YOU STILL CAN." It blew me away to hear Jesus say this. Could I really have the beauty Monique had in my life? Jesus said, "YES," and the best part was that Jesus wanted me to have it and gave it to me. He desired to bless me with my heart's desire, and showed me how He planned on giving it to me in my life. Monique's death meant a lot to me, because Jesus showed me who He is through her. He called her home to be with Him.

She did all that Jesus wanted, living the plan and purpose for her life. Her life was complete, and it was time for her to graduate to Heaven, finding completion in

Christ. She was obedient to all that God called her to. She did not swerve or compromise her faith. She held strong to the end as God calls us all to do in His word. I know she has many blessings in Heaven.

I remember on one occasion doing Monique's makeup on her mother's wedding day, and I can hear her say to me, "I look pale." I didn't think she liked the way I did her makeup and was very surprised when she asked me to do her makeup for the prom. I remember I was putting on her makeup, thinking I cannot wait to have a daughter so that I can do this with her on her prom night and any other time she wants me to. I was blessed to do Monique's makeup that day, and even more blessed that she liked it.

She was a very special young lady. Yes, I admired her when she was with us on earth, and I admire her now being in Heaven. Her youth, beauty, energy, outlook, and zeal, but most of all her witness and faith in Jesus, and how confident she was, not allowing the world or teenage pressures to change her. She was all that God had made her to be and flew with it as high as she could. I pray for and desire a daughter like her, but even if the Lord does not give me a daughter, at least I knew Monique.

Today, I stand strong in my faith with Jesus, remembering Monique and her obedience to Him, as I seek the dreams He has for me this year, and what He wills to give me. Thank you, Sweet Jesus, for Monique, and all you are still doing through her even as she is gone from us, but forever with you! Hallelujah, and again I say, Hallelujah, Glory to God in the Highest!

Lita

Legacy

When I think of Monique, I think of what she did for our God. I think of her maturity, and how she walked in it. I am talking about spiritual maturity, speaking with boldness the Word of God. I have thought about her and the legacy she left for everyone. She is an example to the young and old. This is what I see in Monique Ashley Perez:

M-memory: Proverbs 10:7 (NIV) . . . The memory of the righteous will be a blessing.

O-optimizing: Ephesians 5:15-16 (NIV) . . . Be very careful, then, how you live—not as unwise but as wise, making the most of every opportunity.

N-neutral: 1 Corinthians 9:22 (NIV) . . . To the weak I became weak, to win the weak. I have become all things to all men so that by all possible means I might save some.

I-(her): 1Cor. 3:6 (NIV) . . . I planted the seed, Apollo's watered it, but God made it grow.

Q-Quiet: Matthew 6:1, 6 (NIV) . . . Be careful not to do your 'acts of righteousness' before men, to be seen by them. . . . Then your Father, who sees what is done in secret, will reward you.

U-understanding: Proverb 10:13 (NIV) Wisdom is found on the lips of the discerning . . .

E-example: 1 Timothy 4:12 (NIV) . . . Don't let anyone look down on you because you are young, but set an example for the believers in speech, in life, in love, in faith and in purity.

A-anointed: Isaiah 61:1 (NIV) . . . The Spirit of the Sovereign Lord is on me, because the Lord has anointed me to preach good news to the poor. He has sent me to bind up the brokenhearted,

S-secret: Matthew 6:3-4 (NIV) . . . But when you give to the needy, do not let your left hand know what your right hand is doing, so that your giving may be in secret. Then your Father, who sees what is done in secret, will reward you.

H-humble: James 4:10 (NIV) . . . Humble yourselves before the Lord, and he will lift you up.

L-light: Matthew 5:16 (NIV) . . . In the same way, let your light shine before men, that they may see your good deeds and praise your Father in heaven.

E-excellent: Proverbs 17:27 (NIV) . . . He who has knowledge spares his words, and a man of understanding is of excellent spirit.

Y-your: Matthew 26:39 (NIV) . . . "My Father, if it is possible, may this cup be taken from me. Yet not as I will, but as you will."

P-persecuted: Matthew 5:10 (NIV) . . . Blessed are those who are persecuted because of righteousness, for theirs is the kingdom of heaven.

E-exalted: Matthew 23:12 (NIV) . . . For whoever exalts himself will be humbled, and whoever humbles himself will be exalted.

R-real: 1John 3:18 (NIV) . . . Dear children, let us not love with words or tongue but with actions and in truth. This then is how we know that we belong to the truth, and how we set our hearts at rest in his presence

E-effective: 1 Thessalonians 2:13 (NIV) . . . And we also thank God continually because, when you received the

word of God, which you heard from us, you accepted it not as the word of men, but as it actually is, the word of God, which is at work in you who believe.

Z-zealous: Acts 22:3 (NIV) . . . I was thoroughly trained in the law of our fathers and was just as zealous for God as any of you are today.

Carmen

Chapter Twelve

Memories for a Lifetime

"If anyone speaks, he should do it as one speaking the very words of God. If anyone serves, he should do it with the strength God provides, so that in all things God may be praised through Jesus Christ. To him be the glory and the power forever and ever. Amen."

—1 Peter 4:11 NIV

This Scripture seems to sum-up the way that Monique lived her life. Did she do the normal things other children do? She certainly did. Her brother admits they didn't always get along, but that's the way it is with siblings. Yet he also admits that she tried to bring him closer to God, and that is not typical. Many children often don't think about God very much, except at Christmas and Easter, and then God is often obscured by the commercial hype that surrounds holidays and other special occasions, similar to the way that other fantasy characters are, like Santa Claus, the Easter Bunny, and the Tooth Fairy. Monique was wise beyond her years in knowing that each of us should gift others every day with love, encouragement, a smile, or a song.

Monique had a heart that makes a person wonder how it fit inside her chest. It was so large, filled with love, and overflowing with compassion for everyone she came in contact with—totally opposite from the Grinch's heart, which was three sizes too small. I'm sure that if Monique could tell us, she would wish that every child, teenager, and adult who reads this book, would strive to love God and all those they touch the way she did. Monique was love personified. She never met a person she did not like. If you had a problem, she would try to help you through it. No conflict was too large for her—no person unworthy of experiencing God's love through her offerings.

Jesus asks us to be like Him. Of course, we could never be as perfect as our Lord, but we can strive to be like Him to the best of our ability, and really, that is all He asks. It is okay to stumble and fall occasionally. That is when God picks us up and carries us on His shoulder. He is always there, loving and encouraging us to fight the good fight, and our reward in Heaven will be great!

Chasing Seagulls

I first met Monique when she was really young. She was only in the sixth grade and to be honest, I did not think I liked her very much. But as the years passed, I began to notice there was something very special about her. It helped that I was getting older and could begin to see her for who she really was. It was at the church youth group that we began to see each other differently. We would hang together all the time. Monique's stepdad would say to me, "When are you going to admit that you two have a special relationship?" Of course, I never did, but it was true. Monique meant more to me than anything. I loved her so much.

We use to hang out at the J Street Marina. We went there a lot just to eat and spend time together. One day, we were sitting in my old blue Tercel when Monique started throwing French fries out the car window, and seagulls started appearing to eat the fries. The next thing you knew there was a flock of gulls swarming over the French fries that Monique was feeding them. In their frenzy to eat the fries, the seagulls began to swarm my car! They were even trying to get inside the car. Monique was laughing and screaming at the same time. We started driving away, and as we looked back, the flock of seagulls was chasing us.

Another time when we went to the J Street Marina, Monique ordered a lot of food from McDonald's. I was really surprised at how much she could eat. But that day, she ate a little too much. She had to get out of my car to vomit on the grass. It was really kind of disgusting! The next thing we knew, a group of seagulls showed-up and ate Monique's vomit! It made me kind of sick, but Monique thought it was the funniest thing. She laughed and laughed about it, and then I noticed that she didn't look sick at all.

The Greatest Day of the Year

I had a thought, today. There is only one day better than Christmas. That day is today. It is the most wonderful day of the year because it's your BIRTHDAY! I know you are having a great celebration up in Heaven. Happy B-day Monique. Have an infinite number more to come!

Love, Daniel

Tell Him

I remember when we were in Silhouettes, a singing group at high school. I always was trying to encourage Monique to go up and sing. I knew that one day she would make it big. I especially tried to encourage her to sing a song titled "Tell Him." Monique performed this song with her best friend Beatriz. They finally did it, and it was a show stopper. Monique was awesome. Their duet was the hit of the night. We love Monique, and miss her so much.

Dinora

Cherished Times

I was thinking of all the crazy times we had, Monique. I heard a song today that reminded me about the time when it was Bianca's B-day, and you called channel 93.3 to dedicate one of their songs to her. Man, I miss those days when I would go to your house after church and just hang out and listen to music while our moms drank coffee.

Oh, and you know what else I remember? I remember when my mom made me walk to your house because a piece to our vacuum was missing, and when I got to your front door, I heard Bianca and you laughing and saying, "Wait don't open it yet, Uncle Rick." You ran to your room and acted like you were asleep, but I knew you weren't, and went in your room to peek. Bianca giggled and gave it away! I would give anything to have that day back, but friends don't let friends miss Heaven, right?

Miriam

The Best of Times

It's pretty crazy that it has been four years that you've been out of my life. I remember when we used to go to church on Wednesdays. You used to sing up on stage with Danielle. Those days were the best. I still remember as if it were yesterday. I recall the times when I would go to my aunt's house, and then visit you at your house across the way. Dari and I watched "La Bamba" with you. I can't explain how much I miss you. I can only go and look back at all the memories we shared together. I hope for the day we see each other again.

I want you to know that I LOVE YOU and thank you for everything you have done for me. Thank you for the advice all those times and for giving me rides home when I was stranded at church. Thanks for going to my quinceanera and having such a great time. Now whenever I see my video, I see you having a blast with all of us. When Dari and I went to visit you at the hospital, I thought that you were going be okay, and that you would come out of there like a champ.

I never thought Pebbles would be texting me two weeks later telling me you had died. That was the worst text I ever received. It hurt so bad to even breathe. I am okay now, just missing you. I used to see your family around everywhere before I moved to Hemet. Your mom reminds me so much of you. Both of you laugh exactly the same. Thanks for watching over me and helping me get through the tough stuff. I love you.

Martha

Water Bugs

Down below the surface of a quiet pond lived a little colony of water bugs. They were a happy colony, living far away from the sun. For many months, they were very busy, scurrying over the soft mud on the bottom of the pond. Every once in a while, one of the bugs seemed to lose interest in its friends, clinging to the stem of a pond lily; it gradually moved out of sight and was seen no more.

"Look!" said one of the water bugs. "Our friend is climbing up the lily stalk. Where do you think she is going?"

Up, up, up it slowly went. Even as they watched, the water bug disappeared from sight. Its friends waited and waited, but it didn't return.

"That's funny!" said one of the water bugs. "Wasn't she happy here?" asked a second.

"Where do you suppose she went?" wondered a third.

No one had an answer.

Finally, one of the water bugs gathered its friends together.

"I have an idea. The next one that climbs up the lily stalk must promise to come back and tell us where he or she went, and why."

"We promise," they said solemnly.

One spring day not long after, the water bug who had suggested the plan found himself climbing up the lily stalk. Before he knew what was happening, he had broken through the surface of the water and fell onto a lily pad above. When he awoke, he looked around in surprise. He couldn't believe what he saw. A startling change had come over his old body. Movement revealed four silver wings and a long tail. Even as he struggled, he felt an impulse to move his wings. The warmth of the sun soon dried the moisture from his new body, and as he moved his wings again, he suddenly found himself above the water. He had become a dragon fly! Swooping and dipping in great curves, he flew through the air. He felt exhilarated in his new atmosphere.

Soon, the new dragonfly landed on a lily pad to rest and looked below to the bottom of the pond. Why, he was right above his old friends, the water bugs! There they were, scurrying around, just as he had been doing some time before.

Then the dragonfly remembered his promise. Without thinking the dragonfly darted down. Suddenly, he hit the surface of the water and bounced away. Now that he was dragonfly, he no longer could go into the water.

"I can't return!" he said in dismay. At least I tried. But I can't keep my promise. Even if I could go back, not one of the water bugs would know me in my new body. I guess they will have to wait until they become dragonflies, too. Then they'll understand what happened to me, and where I went."

Unknown

Chapter Thirteen

Letters to Monique

"Blessed are those who have learned to acclaim you, who walk in the light of your presence, O Lord."

—Psalms 89:15 NIV

Most of us are blessed with a few close friendships. Of these, some have a significant influence on our lives for a few days or for many years. Monique had the kind of personality and evangelistic outreach that has spanned many years, starting from her childhood and lasting throughout her short life—and beyond.

As a student, Monique even managed to inspire the teachers and other professionals she came into contact with, including doctors and nurses at the hospital as well as people in her church and those who worked with her in her beloved singing and youth groups. Monique devoted herself to God in every facet of life, especially when it came to showing the Lord how much she loved to sing for Him. She knew how to make a joyful noise unto the Lord!

This book includes testimonies from young folks who give Monique credit for helping them turn their lives around—lives that might have ended tragically had they continued to follow the path they were on before meeting her. She never shied away from leading a fellow student down the righteous path or introducing one to the Lord, even though it might not have been the "in" thing to do.

Monique's family also received gifts from her generous bounty. Parents, grandparents, aunts, uncles, and siblings were continuously amazed at how "grown-up" she was. Monique not only reminded them of God's love, she also showed it, and especially during the times she was like a "little mother" to her brother and sister during the years when I was a single parent. To say we miss her is like saying we would miss the light if the sun stopped shining. I'm just so happy that Monique was able to bring joy and peace to so many in so little time.

Monique,

It's our senior year. I remember telling Karyna and you that I wanted to start my own record label and produce music that would impact the masses and bring them to Christ. Well Monique, the time has come. I am leaving for Orlando to go to music production and business school. I did it! I am so looking forward to this, and have never been so determined. Girl, I miss you a lot. I wish you were here to see what is in store for my future in music. I know that without God, I never would have made it this far. You always encouraged me to try.

Every time I look at your picture, my day goes much smoother. I can hardly believe it, Monique. I am pursuing my dreams. You don't know how much you are missed here, but then again, maybe you do. Life is so different without you. I know we will be together again one day, and walk those streets of gold, and swim in oceans of crystals. I bet you are having so much fun up there chillin' with the angels, singing in the choir. I miss you so much, and I cannot wait to see you once again.

I love you, Monique,
God Bless you,
Carlitos

Monique,

Sometimes you don't realize what you have until you don't have it anymore. I realize this now, and I have a real sense of loss. I will always remember that I had a crush on you. It was easy to have a crush on you because you were the nicest person to me. I remember seeing you at that Christian Center over by Toys R Us. I used to skate. You always tried to get me to go to church as you stood outside, trying to get me to go inside. I remember you were in my sixth-grade class. You would always help me with my homework. I will never forget you.

Luis

Monique,

I really miss you and wish you were still here. You have made me a stronger Christian. After we lost you, it made me want to have the same relationship with God that you had. I am still working on it. I just wish I was working on it with you. I cannot wait to be in the presence of God, standing next to you, just praising Him. I love you so much, and I will see you again someday.

Love you,
Natalie

Monique,

I haven't talked to you in my dreams in a while. I just wanted to let you know that I'm doing pretty well. I finally came out of my shell, as you encouraged me to. I went out and joined ASB. You always told me that I was quiet and shy, and that I should get involved at school. We all miss you at Chula Vista High School. Thanks for being a good friend to me.

Your friend,
Francisco

Hey, Monique,

I miss you so much. Guess what? You make me a little jealous! You're up there in Heaven, waiting for the rest of us believers! Yup, that includes me. Make sure you tell God to let you visit me sometime, and we'll praise and worship together. I mean, that is my passion and yours too, right? Well, I kind of have to because I'm working on my senior portfolio. Lucky you, for two reasons. First, you are in a way better place than us, and second, you don't have to do the portfolio! Love you, Monique!

Unknown

Hi, Monique,

I cannot believe that you are not here to experience everything we've gone through this year, our senior year. It's been hard for me, you know? I mean, I get by, but not that well. I miss telling you everything that happened at home and school.

Monique, I miss you, I really miss you. I still do not want to believe that you are gone. I keep thinking that you just moved to another place, but not forever. Maybe it's because I do not want to accept it. All I know is that I miss you a lot. Monique, you made me laugh, smile, and cry, and you showed me how to live life without a care. But now that you are gone, it has all disappeared. I hope that you are happy where you are now. I really do miss you a lot, little one.

Marissa, Yessenia, Karyna, Martha, a whole bunch of other people, and I want you here with us. Monique, you meant a lot to us. You were beautiful in every way. We will never forget you. Please, don't forget me. Well, Monique, this is it for now. Promise you will look down and guide me toward the right direction—where you are.

I love you,
Betty

Monique,

There are absolutely no words to describe the pain we're feeling. It was such a shock to know that one day you were here, and the next you were taken away from us! I cannot imagine the hardships your parents are faced with. I hope to see you again one day. I just know that God has a plan for you, a plan so great there was no way for you to finish it on earth. I hope you're able to look down on us and see how many people love you. You were an angel on earth, and I know that God has made you one in Heaven! You will be missed. I will see you again one day. Thank you for all your help and for always knowing just what to say. I will miss you so much. I love you.

Love always and forever,
Your friend,
Athena

Monique,

I just stole your comment about virginity! Ha, Ha. How are you? I hope everything is going great for you up in Heaven. Things have been pretty hard, but they are slowly getting better. I can't believe it's nearly four years that you have been gone. It seems like we just hugged each other yesterday.

I remember when we were in Ms. Zazueta's class for math in seventh grade. You were the first friend that I ever made in middle school. You always made me laugh, and we would get in trouble for talking in class. Then in tenth grade, I had you in English class. Every time I needed lotion, you would have it. You have made an awesome difference in my life and in the lives of so many other people. Not just by smiling and being who you are, but by showing us that God is real. I love you, Monique, and think about you everyday. I hope to see you soon. Save me a spot in Heaven.

Karina

Monique,

I miss you so much, and I'm sure you miss us, too. I know you're living the "real" life that you would always talk about. You know being up in Heaven right now making sure all of us are okay down here. You always used to tell me that Karyna and I would end up together, and as always you were right. Sometimes I get the feeling you're making sure that she and I never get into trouble. You still mean so much to me as a friend, because of your beautiful smile and the way you laughed. It turned each of my days into happy ones. There was never one dull moment with you. I wasn't one of the lucky people to see you on your last day back at school to say goodbye one last time, but I still get those feelings that you're always around me.

I guess there really is no need to say goodbye. Thank you for every hint of advice you've ever given me. Thank you for brightening my day with your smile. Thank you for always believing in everything I'd told you I wanted to do, and thank you for being yourself. One last thing, without you, I would be a diffcrent person today. I love you so much, Monique. I can't wait to see you in Heaven.

Angel

Monique,

Well, here we are at the end of our year. I had a lot of fun with you this year. You always had a big smile on your face and made my day. Yup! You sure did! I love you, Monique! I'm pretty sure you know, but I want you to know that I always will remember and love you.

Your second-best friend,

Beatriz

Hey, Monique,

I'm glad I was able to know you. You are the greatest person I've ever known. When I saw you, I could see God in your eyes. I can't wait till I see you again. Love always

Beth

Hey, girl,

I'm really glad I met you this year, even though we didn't talk much. You taught me so much about life. I will miss you and your heart-warming smile. I will see you again one day.

Love,
Alicia

Monique,

It was an honor to have been your president this year in Silhouettes. It's really encouraging to spend time with a person as strong in faith as you. You are an inspiration to all, and you will always be remembered in my heart!

Amanda

Monique,

We're gonna miss you!! I think about you every day! Always remember that I love you forever and ever. We started off wrong, but ended up great friends! You always made me smile and laugh. Take care, and watch over those special people that you love . . . even me, he, he. I love you, sweetie. I'll be with you soon!

XOXO,
Raeanne

Hey, Monique,

It's me, Martha, your sixth-grade buddy! Look, I made it this crazy year! Monique, I never really got to say goodbye, and I don't think I'll ever be able to. All of my memories remain inside with no one to share them with. In my heart, you're still here and in my dreams. You changed my life in so many ways. I wish people could understand how dear you are to my heart. I'll never forget the first day of school at Harbor side. We were both new, but you made friends fast. I was a loner, but you left the others to become my best friend. I love you.

Martha

Hey there, buddy of mine,

Thanks for being a great friend. I still remember when you would sing to me on our way to class sometimes. I wonder if you're singing to me. I know you are and that makes me miss you more. I love you lots. Don't forget the time we had.

Love,
Tanya

Hey, Monique,

You have been a really good friend since middle school. Even though I never got a chance to say that I'll miss you, I'll never forget you. Never forget me.

Love always,
Evelyn

Hey Monique!

Wow! I can't believe this year is over. I'm glad I got to know you a lot better this year! Isn't it weird how time passes so fast? You've been such a great friend, ever since I met you in the seventh grade. You were the first friend I made in a new school! I hope you have a great summer. Be safe. Keep in touch, and never forget me! I know I won't. Te quiero mucho! Hugs and kisses.

Karina

Monique,

Life certainly gives us our twists. Maybe that's good. It's just that I miss you. It's really not fair. I want you back, but really don't want to be selfish. I just wanted to tell you how much you mean to me, but I guess you could tell, right? If not, now you know. I just wish you could be my guardian angel and see me through these hard times. But I had you dear to my heart, and I hope you hold me close to you, too. I know you're one of the stars at night that embraces my sleep. I LOVE YOU!

Ramsey

Hey, Monique,

I'll always remember you. These past years were the best, especially in the eighth grade. I was looking at my eighth-grade yearbook, and on almost every page, you wrote something crazy. Well, keep an eye on me, okay, you crazy girl?

Love,
Karen

Hey, Monique,

This year was great. I had a lot of fun getting to know you. I wish I could have gotten to know you better. Well, during the little time that I had, I found out that you're so sweet and caring. A lot of people say I remind them of you, and that means so much to me because of who you are and what you stand for. I'm gonna miss you. I love you.

Erin, a.k.a. Silhouette sister!

Monique,

I will never forget your beautiful smile, and how you always made me laugh. I now know that you are an angel in Heaven, and God took you to be by his side, so this really isn't a goodbye, but more like a see-you-later

Jessica

Monique,

You made me think of how valuable our friendship was. You were a shining star, and that is how I will always remember you. Keep guard on all those who cared for you. I love you very much, Monique. I will never forget you!

With love,
your second-best friend,
Beatriz

Monique,

Era una persona linda, y muy amable. Siempre tenia una sonrisa, que te ponia en tu cara cuando la mirabas. Era una buena amiga. Siempre que la necesitaba ella siempre estaba ahí para mí. Ahora, esta en un lugar major, esta con dios. Te quiero mucho y nunca te voy a olvidar.

Cesar

Baby,

"You always said we'd graduate together and be big singers one day. You told me to keep my head up, and always remember God loves me. Even though it is incredibly hard and painful for me, I know you are in a better place. I'll keep singing for us, and for our dreams. I'll always love you, monicky!

Karyna

Monique,

No one else can honestly understand why you were the one to leave. I will never forget you, your smile, or your character. Who knows if anyone can ever be equal to you? Your sixth-grade bud,

Martha

Chica,

Thanks for filling our hearts with joy when we needed it. There will always be a place for you in our hearts. But God took you for a reason—to be one of his angels on his side from now on.

Love,
Jorge

Monique,

We lost a star on earth, but we gained a new one in the sky. Monique, you truly were a star, not just on stage but in our hearts. We only knew each other a few months, but we shared lots of memorics. I admired your beautiful voice, great personality, and beauty, but most of all, the ability to cheer-up people on their worst day. Even when you had a bad day, you were always there with your big, goofy smile, calling everyone a dork. I'm gonna miss that, running up to me, hugging me, catching-up in the halls. But I know that someday, we'll walk again through the halls—the halls of Heaven, and we'll catch-up on everything we've missed.

To me, you'll always be my shining star—the star that shines the brightest, the one who is most likely singing her way through the halls of Heaven, singing to the angels. I LOVE YOU, and don't forget me.

Melissa

Monique,

I will miss but NEVER FORGET YOU. You will always be with me, in my heart, my dreams, and my memories. I LOVE YOU! Always yours,

Tony

Monique,

"Beautiful," "sweet," and "kind" described Monique Perez. She was an angel sent to us, so perfect and innocent. Although words cannot describe her beauty and kindness, we will never lose the unforgettable moments when she changed our days for the better, or the way her smile would light your day. It's hard to realize she is no longer with us. We must not dwell on the sadness of her death, but on all those wonderful times she touched our hearts.

Crystal

Monique,

Thank you for all the times you made me smile when it wasn't my best day, and for all the memories you left. I love you.

Dolores

I know I'll never meet anyone as nice and beautiful as you. I miss you, and I love you so much.

Marissa

Monique is the definition of how everyone should be. She always had a smile on her face, and always was there when you needed a shoulder to cry on. I love you, Monique. You will be in our hearts, forever.

Karina

Monique was the type of person that when you were sad, she would bring a smile to your face with just her smile.

Angelique

She was the person who made the world a better place. She will be missed and never forgotten. I love you, Monique. Thanks for all those good times we shared.

Yessenia

Monique,

I'm so glad I got to know you over the years. I remember when we were in the Scrapbook Club together in middle school. Now that we are apart, I will miss you, truly. But you will always live in my heart. You have made a great impact on my life. When you left, it made me realize that I can't take life for granted. I have to live life to the fullest. That's exactly what you did. I'll see you when I get up there. I hope you will remember me. Save me a spot in Heaven. I love you, always and forever.

Unknown

Monique,

You were such a good friend. We used to chit-chat outside class. You always seemed to know how to pick-up everyone's day with your good advice, and even just your smile. Thank you for always being there for me when I needed you the most. I wish your family the best of luck. You were truly a good friend, daughter, sister, etc. I remember we had a conversation in fifth period when I asked you, "What's the worst thing you ever did?" You said, "Sneak out of the house." But I love you, and I will always keep you in my memories and my heart. I am sending my love to your family as well. Love you, always.

Dolores

Don't ever abandon me. Be my guide and my eyes from up so high. I need the sound of your voice. I'm sorry. I just miss you so much.

Smelly Mely

Hey girl,

What can I say? I barely started writing, and I'm already crying. Thanks for being there and for caring so much. You're a very caring person—so lovable, and not just to me but too many. Every time I walk to second period, it's hard, because you were usually there, waiting for me with a big smile and hug. You know, I really need you right about now. I need someone to talk to, and to hold my hand and tell me everything is going to be all right. You were the only one who could take everything and make it fine again. Love you.

Melissa

Monique,

I didn't know you as well as I had hoped, but I did get a chance to talk and see you at the Christmas party. You had an "air" about you that showed so much love and compassion. Thanks for blessing me with your smile.

Amanda

Ever so dearest Monique,

Where to begin? I miss you and love you; that is basically how I feel. Thanks so much for your guidance when I needed it. This is so hard. I don't know when I will see you again, but I know that we will meet up again someday. The memories we had will forever be with me. That laugh, how I'm going to miss that laugh. Yessenia! You'd call my name in the hallways. I'd give anything to hear your voice again. It was an honor to meet such a pure soul! I will never forget you. I love you so much! May Heaven be everything you expected.

Love always,
Yessenia

Ever so dearest Monique,

I don't know where to begin. Let me start by saying that I feel truly blessed to have had such an incredible person in my life. We became so close in such a short period of time. You were like a sister to me. I always knew I could confide and trust in you. I found comfort in your arms. My life will never be the same because you were a part of it. I love you so much, sweet angel. Save me a spot next to you and my baby cousin in Heaven. One sweet day, we will be together again . . . forever.

Love,
Karyna

Hey Monique,

Dang, this year is over. Time passes so fast. I'm so glad I knew you. You made a big difference in my life. There isn't a day when I don't thank you for the blessings you brought into my life. I love you and will always. I wish your family the best, and I know you're looking-out for all that love you. I'm not saying goodbye, but I'll see you, because I will see you again. Well once again I love you, and will always keep you in my heart.

Love

Hey Monique!

It's been great knowing you for the past three years. There's not one day I don't think about you. I miss you so much, sweetie! I will never forget you and our memories. I hope you're looking over us up there!

Love,
Gaby

Monique,

Hey sweetie! Man, it's been the best time knowing you! It's going to be hard going through life without you.

We miss and love you so much! We'll never stop thinking about you! You were such a big part of our hearts, and now you're gone. We miss you, sweet angel!

Love you,
Erica

Monique,

It's been good knowing you. I just wish we could have talked more. I will miss you, but I know you are in a better place.

Love,
Yvette

Monique,

We'll miss you a lot! I miss having boy-talks with you. I wish you the best in Heaven! I hope you're watching over us. Oh, and thank you for saying goodbye to me! I'll never forget you. You'll always be a part of me in a very special way. I love you and your beautiful soul! You'll always be in mi Corazon! Te quiero, Monique Ashley Perez.

Love,
Andrea

Monique,

I will always remember your sweet spirit and kind heart. Thank you for being such an important part of all our choirs. There will always be a part of you in room 506!

Love always,
Mrs. Schroeder

Hey, what's up, Monique? I just wanted to tell you that I love and miss you so much. I always loved your smile. I love you. I'll see you when the time is right.

I LOVE YOU! Stephanie

Monique,

I love you and miss you so much. I think about you every day. Thanks for being a part of my life. Star power! I love you.

Leissa

Monique,

I just wanted to tell you that even though you can't hear me, I love you, and we do miss you. I'm so happy to know you are where you wanted to be. I want to thank you for being so great! Thank you for bringing me back to Jesus! You are the best. You have truly fulfilled my life by taking me to church. Thanks! I love you so much! Monique, I love you!!

Tamara

Monique,

I remember sitting in class, and every time I saw you, you were always smiling. If you weren't smiling, you were probably smiling on the inside, because you would get in trouble for laughing. You were the type that would observe a lot, and watch everyone carefully. I know, because I would, too. You would try to find something good in everybody.

I remember at a Silhouettes get-together, it was Jessica, you, and I talking about guys, and how you wish you could ask your mom if you could go out with your boyfriend. But they wouldn't let you because of your age. I was listening and trying to understand. I wish, well actually, I always wanted to get to know you more than I did. We were friends, but not as close as I would have wished. Jessica would talk to you and about you, and I always wished, deep down inside, to have something like the same relationship as you and Jessica had. No one will ever forget you. We'll always have you in our hearts. I know you can't talk to me. You can't read this, but you know what I wanted to say for the longest time. I love you.

Andrea

Hey Monique,

I just want to say thanks for being a cool person. It was great knowing you. I will always remember you as the happy person you are. I know that you're in a better place, so keep an eye on us.

Dustin

As the days go by I will remember you
always. As the days go by the pain will
ease slowly.
As the days go by I will pray for you.
As the days go by life will go on.
And no matter how much I wish you were
here, I know deep inside you will always be
near.
As the days go by you will be in my heart,
For nothing in this world could tear us
apart.
As the days go by I will not say good-bye
and I will not cry.
As the days go by I grow closer to being
with you again.
So as the days go by my beloved friend,
save me a spot next to you up in Heaven….

Your Friends that Miss you!

The Holy Spirit

Monique had been complaining of headaches since February. You took her to the doctor, and she was diagnosed with migraine headaches. She was given a schedule to follow, and a dietary log to document the food she had eaten and the times she had headaches.

Then it was April 1st. The kids had just started spring break. To your surprise, Monique said she wanted to go with Jacob and Bianca to her grandparents'. The reason you were so surprised was that Monique always had a lot going on. It had been a few years since she had been able to go and just have a vacation with her grandparents. Even your parents were surprised when you called and told them that Monique would be going to their home for vacation. They were so excited. You asked Monique if she was sure, and she said that she felt she needed to get away.

I could see she was going through some stressful teenage stuff. You drove her to your parents' home that weekend. Your parents were going to bring the kids back on Easter weekend. When you left to return to San Diego, everything seemed fine. You called Monique, and she said that she was tired and she just wanted to sleep. She felt bad because she thought her grandparents felt she did not want to get out of bed and spend time with them. But you were soon to discover that something was wrong.

On Monday, April 5th, Monique called you at work. As soon as she heard your voice, she started crying. The moment you heard her voice, the mother in you knew there was something wrong. She told you she wanted to come home, that she missed you, and was not feeling well. You told her you would be there first thing the next morning.

The morning came so very quickly. You and Bill went straight to your parents' home to pick up the kids. When you saw Monique, she started crying, and I saw you hug her, just like you had hugged her a thousand times before.

Bill woke the other kids and told them they were going home. Monique said she was feeling bad. She felt that everyone was mad at her because she wanted to come home. But it wasn't like her to disappoint others. On the way home, she kept asking you to put on a song called, "I Can Only Imagine." You knew it was one of her favorite songs. You didn't think much about it at the time, but she asked you again and again to play it over and over. You watched her through the rear-view mirror. She had her head leaning against the window, staring out to the heavens. You had this uneasiness about you so you asked her if you could hear something else.

When you arrived home, you kept envisioning her looking out the window. It reminded you of a conversation you and Monique had a few weeks earlier. The two of you were listening to that song, and there was a line that talks about walking in the Son. She asked you, "Mom, what do you think the song means by walking in the Son?" Do you think it means walking in the sun or Son? You said walking in the Son. She said, "Yeah, me, too." You couldn't shake that conversation and kept seeing her staring out the window on the way back home. That vision was so persistent, I saw you struggling, trying to break free of it.

Monique was taking a nap when suddenly she awoke, came out of her room, and asked if she could go to band practice. She was the lead singer of the youth band.

Wednesday night, the youth band was going to play in the main sanctuary. Lydia, I heard you ask Monique if she was sure she was feeling up to it. She said "yeah." So, you took her to practice. Everyone was surprised to see her since they knew she had been out of town. When she returned home, she said she had a good time and almost seemed as though nothing was wrong.

Right before you went to work, Monique called you and said she did not think she could make it to the Wednesday service. I could see that she was not feeling well and had been complaining of nausea. I heard her tell you that she would call the leaders and let them know. When you got home, she was lying down and said she still felt bad. You had to teach in the children's church that night, so Bill said he would stay with her. You thought she would probably sleep all night, so you went to church. When you got home you went into her room to see if she was asleep. You carefully tiptoed into her room just to check on her. As you walked out, she called you and asked how the band did. You said they did fine.

She asked, "Are you sure, because I know on the song I sing, the band struggles slightly." Then she laughed, and you said, "It was fine." The next morning was Wednesday, April 8th, the day the very structure of your family would be altered forever. When you and Bill awoke, Monique was not feeling well, so you called Kaiser at to make an appointment. They said they could see her at 9:00 a.m. You thought it was going to be a routine appointment, so Bill said he would take her, since he was on vacation. Lydia, you had to inspect a house in Coronado, and you needed to trade cars with Bill.

You called Bill at Kaiser to switch cars. Bill called you

and said that the doctors needed to talk to the two of us. Lydia, you did not think much about it at the time. When you arrived; Bill was leaning on a pole outside Kaiser. The look on Bill's face was not what you expected. As you approached him, his face was overcome by paleness as dots of sweat made his forehead their home. I saw your strength, Lydia, as you would not be moved by what you saw.

You and Bill met with the doctor. The doctor looked at you and paused, seemingly to find the right words, she said, "Your daughter is very sick." You looked her straight in the eye, somewhat confused, as your world began to come to a screeching halt. The doctor said, "She took additional blood because she could not find exactly what was going on. The tests came back, Monique had leukemia." The tears began to roll down your face, Lydia. You looked at Bill and you could tell by his face this was serious.

The doctor said that Monique was going to be admitted into the hospital a.s.a.p. The doctor said she could tell Monique, but we had to go in with her. Lydia, I covered you with my love and anointed you with supernatural strength. You said, "No, I will tell her." From the moment we walked into the room, your words were carefully chosen. You knew how important it was to speak words of life rather than death. When Monique saw you, she looked straight into your face and asked, "Why are you crying, Mom."

Lydia, you went to her bedside, just as you had done a thousand times over the years and said, "No matter what, God's word is final." Lydia spoke with such confidence, "What I am going to tell you, and no matter what the doctor's report says, we are going to stand on our faith and God's word." Lydia, with such courage, you said, "Monique, the doctors think you have leukemia." Monique looked at you, Lydia, and said, "Is that bad?"

You looked at her and said that we weren't going to think about it more than we had to. For the next thirty days, it seemed like you and your family, were living in a surreal world, and that you would awaken to find that this was nothing more than a nightmare. May 1st was a day that never happened; you prayed the sun would rise in the morning, and you and your family would awaken from this horrible nightmare to finding the integrity of your family secure, to find your Monique beautiful, whole, and ready to go about God's business.

"Safe in God's arms

To be absent from the body is to be in the Presence of the Lord."

—Corinthians 5:8 NIV

On May 1st, 2004, you woke to the sound of Monique crying. She did not feel well and said she wanted to go back to the hospital. She was taken to the Emergency Room where they admitted her instantly. Bill, Lydia, and Bianca were in the emergency room with her. Jake and Nathan had gone to their lacrosse game with their coach. The doctors on duty could not determine exactly what was wrong. She had no fever. There was no need for blood or platelets. They called the oncology department, and they suggested admitting her for the night just for observation. I heard you think to yourself that perhaps Monique's discomfort was due to side effects from the chemotherapy. While waiting for a room, Monique had her eyes closed for a while, and then she turned and looked at Bianca and said, "You are a good sister, Munchkin.

You're the best, and I love you very much, and don't ever forget that."

Bianca looked at her and said, "No, you're the best." Since Monique was going to be admitted, Bill took Bianca home, and you called your parents to come down and help. Bill also went to pick-up the boys from their game. Lydia, you stayed with Monique as you had for the past month, waiting for the doctor to let you know when a room was ready. You kept trying to tell her to get some sleep. She tossed and turned so much. She said that all she wanted to do was sleep. She closed her eyes and was still for a while. Monique appeared asleep when suddenly she opened her eyes, looked at you, and in the most angelic, sincere voice said, "Mom, I really love Isaac." You said, "I know, baby." Isaac was Monique's unofficial boyfriend. I often heard Bill say that Isaac was better than medicine for Monique. This thought was echoed by the nursing staff at Children's Hospital.

She closed her eyes as you sat by her bed. Finally, the nurse said they had a room. Monique kept saying her chest hurt, and she needed something for the pain. As soon as the nurse got her into bed and her IV connected, they came in with the pain medication. She sat up and took the medicine just fine. She lay down and closed her eyes. Bill had just gotten back from taking the kids home, and

Monique started saying how she had to go to the bathroom. She did not want to wait for the nurse so Bill picked her up and carried her into the bathroom.

When Bill lifted Monique she said, "Dad." Bill said, "Yes, Monique." With the most lucid response and looking directly at Bill in the doorway to the bathroom, Monique said, "Not you, my Heavenly Dad." Bill laid her back down, and it looked like she finally was sleeping peacefully. Lydia was resting in the chair next to her, and Bill was at the foot of her bed. Suddenly, she opened her eyes and said to you, Lydia, "Mom, let's pray." Lydia, you said, "Okay, for what?" She said for the kids on this floor, their parents, everything. "It doesn't matter. I just want to pray."

"My daughter, what a blessing you are in the midst of trial to consider the welfare of others." Lydia nuzzled close to Monique and started praying. She put her hand out, and you grabbed it and kept praying. Suddenly, she let go of your hand and started praying in spirit. I know you could not understand. Then she called out, "Jesus, Jesus," and she put her hands straight up, and started singing, "Jesus, lover of my soul." My daughter, Lydia, I counted all your tears. I felt the pain in your heart, as you did not want to admit what you knew was happening.

You started calling out to Monique and told her to put her hands down. As I collected your tears, you said, "Monique, no." She turned and looked at you with the most peaceful look on her face and said, "Mom, you can hear me?" At that moment you went to get the nurse. They checked her blood pressure. It was so low, Bill had them re-check it, but it remained extremely low. You went to the bathroom down the hall to pull yourself together. Bill sat in a chair in full assurance and belief that everything would be okay.

You were walking back to the room when you saw the CHET team (Children's Hospital Emergency Team) rolling her bed down the hall to the PICU floor. You closely followed them, but you couldn't go in at this point. You had to wait in the hall. The PICU doctors would come out periodically to give you and Bill updates. Until 7 p.m., they were reasonably sure they would be able to stabilize her. After a couple of hours, which seemed like forever to you, the doctor came out and told us we could go in, but basically, they were having a difficult time stabilizing her. I heard you firmly rebuke his words as you and Bill walked into the observation room. It was a scene that I could not prepare you for. There were so many people there, gallantly fighting to save your Monique's life. Standing in the adjacent room, watching this incredible life-saving effort, you kept repeating to yourself that you would not be moved by what you saw.

Faith was never a question. The God that you serve is a God of miracles, and with one word, He could turn this whole situation around. The doctor came in at one point and asked if you wanted them to perform CPR when it was needed. Then at 9:20, they said, "Do you want us to start CPR now?" You walked out and went into a small room. You knew in your heart that your most precious Monique had gone home to be with the Lord. Even though your faith never wavered, you knew that in a second everything could change. Your wonderful, beautiful Monique had graduated from this world to a world where pain, hurt, and human desire no longer exist.

Legacy

Today, our hearts continue to long for Monique. We know that Jesus was able to take a catastrophic situation and turn it to good. Through Monique, we were allowed to experience a glimpse of eternity. We were given the revelation that Heaven is a real place. Today through Jesus Christ, the seeds Monique planted while on earth continue to produce the sweetest fruit. Many people who never knew Jesus, or simply refused to know him, have come to accept Jesus as their personal savior. What a wonderful legacy, Monique has left behind—to know that so many of her dearest friends and acquaintances have come to know Jesus. The legacy that Monique established will be passed-on for generations to come. Today our Monique has her heart's desire, to dwell in Heavenly mansions, to walk upon streets of gold, splashing in living waters in the presence of God almighty.

We hope it is a great comfort for you to know that years to us are but a moment to Jesus, and that in a twinkling of an eye, we also will be in Heaven, reunited with our loved ones. Our loved ones, who have passed away in Christ, are merely asleep. Jesus promises that those asleep in Christ will be reawaken, that not a single person will be forsaken. What a wonderful event to look forward to, being reunited with our loved ones in Christ. It is a revelation to our family and we hope for yours also, that our loved ones are not only memories, they are our future.

From our family to yours, be very confident that life is short, eternity is forever and Heaven does exist.

For his Glory

Bill & Lydia Maeda and Family

Conclusion

Learning to be more Christ-Like

"Whoever tries to keep his life will lose it, and whoever loses his life will preserve it."

—Luke 17:33 NIV

Although death can feel like it is the end of life, life continues afterward but in a spiritual way. When we learned in Scripture that our bodies are made in the likeness of God, it wasn't the physical body the writer spoke about. It is the spiritual body—the one in which we will meet our Savior, the one that although the physical form dies and withers away, remains alive for all eternity.

As powerful as Monique's testimony and friendship were on earth, they have not diminished, but continue to inspire and encourage others even though she has passed. It is impossible to read this book and not be moved, and I believe that readers will be positively influenced as they learn of the many inspirational acts Monique performed. The fact that she was merely a child makes her life even more wondrous. You cannot help thinking that if one so young influenced so many, so strongly, what can I accomplish?

Each one of us, regardless if we are young or old, should strive to make a positive impact for Christ on each other. That doesn't mean you have to preach. Actions speak louder than words. Like Monique, we can make this impact with a listening ear, kind words, smiles, and plenty of laughs. Kindness is a powerful thing, and it comes from our love of one another. There are so many lost and hurting souls in this world that heaven longs to rescue. Maybe they struggle because the issues of life are so overwhelming. Maybe they are battling physical or mental illness.

Whatever their needs, an act of kindness can go a long way toward making their day a little brighter. It is a simple way to show others how much Jesus loves them: A hug, a smile, words of encouragement, being there for someone who is experiencing a bad day or going through a crisis. By expressing our love and offering acts of kindness, we behave in a Christ-like manner and show others just how much God loves them. We are the Lord's most powerful emissaries on earth. If we can strive each day to act more like our Savior, Jesus Christ, we can turn our sinful world into a kinder, gentler place.

Yes, there are those too immersed in evil to change. Jesus warned us about them. But many others are not evil, simply on the wrong path or stumbling around like a lost lamb. Those are the people we can turn back to God through our simple acts of faith through kindness, a smile, or an uplifting word. Anger only begets anger, hatred, and violence. It turns the soul into a miasma of confusion and self-hatred, and destroys the beauty within. Make a pledge to yourself and God. Start small, if necessary, with a smile and a cheery word. Before long, you, too, can have a powerful effect on other people. Just like Monique.

Well, It's up to You

***"For God so loved the world that He gave
His only begotten Son, that whoever
Believes in Him should not perish but have
everlasting life"***

-John 3:16 NIV

When life has all been said and done, it has always been up to you. God gives us the right to make decision for ourselves, Good decision or not so good decisions. God gives us freewill to choose him or to not choose him. If you would like to live the life that Monique lived here on Earth as well as the life she now lives in Heaven, it is just a heartfelt decision away. You have been given the opportunity to secure your eternity today. Today you are given the unique opportunity to reserve your place in heaven, on the right-hand side of God, for all of eternity Pray this simple prayer and you to will walk on streets of gold and dwell in heavenly mansions.

Father God today I come before in name of your dear son. I confess before you that I have sinned greatly and have fallen short of the glory of God. Today I place my sins before you and ask for your forgiveness. I confess that you are the one and only Son of God, that you willing died on the cross for my sins and arose from the dead three days later. I boldly decree and declare in the mighty name of Jesus, that I am saved today, that I am born again. Father God I stand before you today with great humbleness and supernatural boldness as I confess before you, the

Almighty God, and all of mankind, that I am yours today and yours for all of eternity.

If you prayed this prayer, we would like to welcome you to the family of God. Today you have established a legacy that will also go on from generation to generation. Today you have secured your rightful place in Heaven. Today you will no longer be a memory to your family but you now represent their future. We would love to hear from you, please feel free to contact us and share with us your testimony.

Today
Forget the former things, Do not dwell in the past. See! I am doing a new thing! Now it springs up, I am making a way in the wilderness and streams in the wasteland

Isaiah 43:18

I never thought in my wildest dreams that my daughter would be anything but healed. With my son Jacobs head in my lap asking, will Monique be ok? Of course, Monique will be fine, Monique is already healed in the name of Jesus. The fact of the matter is Monique was not healed on this earthly globe, where we get up to see beautiful sunrises and God created sunsets. But Monique was made whole and perfected in the heavenly realms, seated in the presence of the Almighty God.

So many years have come and gone since our daughter Monique graduated to the heavenlies. What a mind blower it is to know that our daughter resides in the presence of God Almighty.

The scripture above reminds us and encourages us not to look back, not to live in the past, for contemplating the past, prevents us from reaping the rewards God has for us in the present and the future yet to come.

Many years have come and gone since our book was first published in 2011. Many changes have occurred in our lives over the past decade. Lydia and I are now without our parents, that we grew up and entrusted our whole existence to. Parents who protected us and shielded us from life's offerings, the good and the bad. My dad William passed away many years ago. My mom Tsurumi passed away just a year ago. Lydia's dad Tony passed away several years ago, and Lydia's mom Mary just months before my mom. There has been so much loss to consider. There have been many friends and family members who have passed on as well. It seems like the older you get, the more funerals you get to go to and the more eulogies you may be asked give.

Drama, what a concept. I believe we have seen more than our share of this insanity. I think if people realized just how short life is, they wouldn't make so much time for drama. They would pick their battles and choose which battle is really worth fighting for. Yet we seem to have to be so prideful. We seem to have to defend ourselves at all cost. I call this ignorance or just plain foolish pride. I wish in my lifetime to no longer experience this prideful drama. But as I sit here and consider all that has happened, my life could be significantly worse. We as human beings often gauge the quality of our lives based on the quality of the lives of our family and friends. A person I know has said, "Why do Non-Christians have such easier lives." "Why do Non-Christians seem to have everything that I want, but don't have." The really cool thing Monique would say, "So what if you don't have all these things, you can't take them with you." Your relationship you have with Christ can never be taken from you. How insightful for a young girl and old soul. But considering my life, I actually have a pretty good life. I have a wife who loves me, even though I don't talk much, I'm actually kind of a quiet guy, who doesn't say a lot, which could lend itself to not communicating as well as I should. So plainly saying, I don't make it easy. Lydia still loves me. I have a pretty good income, considering I'm retired and draw social security and my retirement check. My wife and I, even at our age, are considering becoming homeowners. But for all the things we would want, the thing we would want the most, the thing we can't have on this earth, our daughter Monique.

So, we are back here again, what has happened since the initial publication of Legacy. We moved out of San Diego. We have 5 grandchildren. I have retired from the Sweetwater Union High School district, where I worked for 30 years. My wife Lydia and I have celebrated our 22nd wedding anniversary.

I have wondered so many times, would life, be different if we never lost our daughter. This is a question where there is no answer. To live our lives asking "What if this or what if that". Even though we have asked that question, more often than we care to admit, we just can't live like that. Too live our lives in a world of what if's, is a life we cannot live.

To not consider the what if's in our life is so very hard. I think nearly impossible. When the prophet Isaiah says don't consider the former things, he means it, but he probably never lost a daughter to leukemia. Still, we plug in and continue to do the best we can. Dealing with the loss has gotten somewhat easier since the years have marched along. But the loss, the hole we live with, will never be filled. But we choose to live with the beautiful memories of our Monique, rather than the what if's. So, for all of you who have been there with us over years. Those who have loved and supported us, we love and support you back. We are all 13 years older, and I would like to believe 13 years wiser. Some of you are no longer with us, I think of passing on as a promotion. For those who are no longer with us. You were just in a graduating class before us. So, we say be blessed and perhaps in another 13 years, maybe another chapter.

> Be still and know that you are loved
> Be still and know that you are blessed
> Be still and know that I am God
> Monique you gone but never forgotten

— Bill Maeda —

Hope-yes there is….

To console those who mourn in Zion, to give them beauty for ashes, the oil of joy for mourning, the garment for praise for the spirit of heaviness; that they may be called trees for righteousness, the planting of the Lord. That He may be glorified.

Isaiah 61:3

Two decades have passed since May 1, 2004; This was the day my daughter Monique went home to be with the Lord. This was totally unexpected and it changed my life. If anybody back then would have told me that I would be where I am today, It would have been impossible for me to accept. I would have thought there is no possible way. I couldn't even think of what the next day would be like. How do you move forward when the situation or circumstance right in front of you makes no sense. It was the most challenging time of my life. My biggest question was "why?" I believed as a family we would serve God together, share the gospel, be an ambassador for Christ and show others God's love, forgiveness and faithfulness through our lives. Now it seemed all stripped away.

Sometimes, like now as I am writing this, it can feel as though it was just yesterday, having to experience all the feelings that came tumbling down on me that day. Having to accept what happened, it was real. Having to face my other children and tell them as well as my parents what happened that night, when we got home from the hospital. It has only been by God's strength, mercy and grace not only that I have been able to move forward with everyday life but I have been able to do what I know God has been directing me to do and that is to share my story. This is the truth, I learned to embrace. This is not the way I wanted our story of serving God as a family to go, I envisioned a much different story line but this is my story.

It took quite a few years for us to have the original book published. It was published in 2011 when everything finally worked itself out and we decided to go forward with the book. It was not easy. Every story had its share of tears and smiles which brought feelings of joy, pain and hurt all at the same time. It was also during this time true healing began, not just putting one foot in front of the other and getting through the day but putting total trust in God, not leaning on my own understanding but knowing God was with me, He promises to never leave us or forsake us.

A new Journey began for me a new deeper and intimate relationship with Jesus. When the idea of putting the book together first started it was to honor my daughter Monique. The stories were so beautiful and heartfelt, we as a family decided her story needed to be told. It was our family desire for all to see a faithful God and what He could accomplish through one young life. A young girl, a young life that was willing to surrender her life completely, wholeheartedly and selflessly, whom I had the privilege to be chosen by God to be her mother. If God can do this through one young life, imagine not only what He could do but wants to do through every generation. My hope is her life will be an encouragement to many and to all those who read this will know we are created for such a time as this.

As I look back over the past years, I now can see God's hand on my life and my family's life. There are still days of hurt and sadness, there are also days of joy. There were many trails we went through but God never let us go. For every sad day there are twice as many happy days of remembering all the good times we had, for every tear I cry there are twice as many happy tears of all the wonderful memories, for all the why's I have there seems to be a letter, email or text of someone telling me they just read her book or they shared her book with someone. Sometimes I meet some after all these years that will tell me a story of Monique.

My children are flourishing, they love God, they each have their own stories of walking through this journey and they have hearts to serve God and others. I am now a grandmother of 5 wonderful, active, loving and precocious grandchildren, which is what I consider one of life's highest honors. Recently we decided to make a big move and left our home town of San Diego and moved two hours away to a new city. I thought I was ready to retire but God again had other plans. I now have a job that I am enjoying and we found a church that me and my husband are both actively involved in. God's plans are definitely greater than ours. I am surrounded by new communities, new opportunities to continue to share my daughter's legacy and hopefully lead others to Christ so they can live a life full of joy, as Monique did. I continue in the Journey set before me and God continues to write my story, even though I still have questions, and I still miss my daughter daily.! I know now she is part of my future, I will see her again and God continues to write my story. He has given me Beauty for Ashes.

In our decision to rebrand the book I am reminded of how many lives Monique has touched, how boldly she shared the gospel and how she genuinely loved God and loved people. It is my prayer that this book will continue to keep Monique's memory alive and will continue to touch future generations to come. I pray that through this book they will continue to see all the lives Monique touched both young and old and that her life could be an example of how no matter the age you can live a life surrendered to Jesus.

If you are a mom who may have gone through the same situation as I or any given situation that would have brought heartbreak and pain. I want you to know that your feelings are real and God knows exactly what you're going through. God created you and he knows you better than anyone else. Most importantly He goes before us, and he makes a way where there seems to be no way. Even though your situation may be difficult and you are brought to a place of hopelessness, Hold on to Jesus even if it is only by the hem of his robe.

If you are a teen or young adult currently reading this book, Jesus loves you and he has a plan for you. You also can love Jesus, live for Jesus and have your very own personal intimate relationship with Jesus. Whether you realize it or not you are impacting those around you, someone is always watching you. You are being an influence in one way or another, so the question isn't will you effect change in others, the real question is will your actions honor God, will your life be a reflection of Jesus.

My hope and prayer is that you are encouraged by this book, that you too will choose to live a life of faith, hope and love. I want to leave you with something Monique would always say and her life is a testimony of it. She would say, "remember what Jesus did for you on the cross" Stay "Crossed Eyed"

> ***Looking to Jesus, the founder and***
> ***perfecter of our faith, who for the joy that***
> ***was set before him endured the cross,***
> ***despising the shame, and is seated at the***
> ***right hand of the throne of God Hebrews***
> ***12:2***

— Lydia Maeda —

About the Authors

Bill & Lydia met in 2001 while both were attending World Harvest Christian Center. They were married in 2002. Bill was serving on the praise and worship team and Lydia was serving in the women's ministry and teaching in children's church. Once married, God directed them to establish a middle school ministry. They helped to establish the youth ministry at the church they were attending, serving in that ministry for two years.

Their daughter, Monique passed in 2004. There would be many challenges, personal and private. With God's grace, mercy and restoring power, they are now serving in one of the largest churches in San Diego, where they reside with their children.

Your Personal Invitation

Each of us has a story to tell, after sharing our story with you we would like you to share your story with us. No story is too big nor is any story to small. Whether a story of triumph, perceived defeat, victory, restoration or a life changing testimony, take a moment and share your testimony or story with us.

To contact Lydia and Bill Maeda
You may visit us at

Website Address: www.legacylivethedifference.com
Facebook: legacylivethedifference
Instagram: legacylivethedifference

www.ingramcontent.com/pod-product-compliance
Lightning Source LLC
Chambersburg PA
CBHW040756120726
48005CB00012B/1192